LLVM Essentials

Become familiar with the LLVM infrastructure and start using LLVM libraries to design a compiler

Suyog Sarda

Mayur Pandey

[PACKT] open source*
PUBLISHING   community experience distilled

BIRMINGHAM - MUMBAI

LLVM Essentials

First published: December 2015

Production reference: 1021215

Published by Packt Publishing Ltd.
Livery Place
35 Livery Street
Birmingham B3 2PB, UK.

ISBN 978-1-78528-080-1

www.packtpub.com

Credits

Authors
Suyog Sarda

Mayur Pandey

Reviewer
Renato Golin

Commissioning Editor
Nadeem Bagban

Acquisition Editor
Harsha Bharwani

Content Development Editor
Priyanka Mehta

Technical Editor
Ryan Kochery

Copy Editor
Imon Biswas

Project Coordinator
Izzat Contractor

Proofreader
Safis Editing

Indexer
Tejal Daruwale Soni

Production Coordinator
Aparna Bhagat

Cover Work
Aparna Bhagat

About the Authors

Suyog Sarda is a professional software engineer and an open source enthusiast. He focuses on compiler development and compiler tools. He is an active contributor to the LLVM open source community. Suyog was also involved in code performance improvements for the ARM and X86 architectures. He has been a part of the compiler team for the Tizen project. His interest in compiler development lies more in code optimization and vectorization.

Previously, he has authored a book on LLVM, titled *LLVM Cookbook* by Packt Publishing.

Apart from compilers, Suyog is also interested in Linux Kernel Development. He has published a technical paper titled *Secure Co-resident Virtualization in Multicore Systems by VM Pinning and Page Coloring* at the IEEE Proceedings of the 2012 International Conference on Cloud Computing, Technologies, Applications, and Management at the Birla Institute of Technology, Dubai. He has earned a bachelor's degree in computer technology from the College of Engineering, Pune, India.

I would like to thank my family and friends for encouraging me to write this book. I am thankful to my co-author and reviewers who did a tremendous job of refining the contents. I would also like to thank the LLVM open source community for always being helpful. It has been a great experience to interact with the community. It is amazing to see how fast LLVM has evolved.

Mayur Pandey is a professional software engineer and open source enthusiast focused on compiler development and tools. He is an active contributor to the LLVM open source community. He has been a part of the compiler team for the Tizen project and has hands-on experience of other proprietary compilers.

He has earned a bachelor's degree in Information Technology from Motilal Nehru National Institute of Technology, Allahabad, India. Currently, he lives in Bengaluru, India.

I would like to thank my family and friends who made it possible for me to complete the book by taking care of my other commitments, and who have always being encouraging.

About the Reviewer

Renato Golin has worked with toolchains since 2008, developing debuggers and compilers for multiple languages and platforms, and has also been LLVM Tech Lead at ARM and Linaro, focusing on code generation, correctness, performance, and providing a complete toolchain solution based on LLVM for the diverse ARM platforms.

Before that, he spent a decade moving between web back-ends, databases, distributed systems, big data and bioinformatics, always working on and with open source projects.

www.PacktPub.com

Support files, eBooks, discount offers, and more

For support files and downloads related to your book, please visit www.PacktPub.com.

Did you know that Packt offers eBook versions of every book published, with PDF and ePub files available? You can upgrade to the eBook version at www.PacktPub.com and as a print book customer, you are entitled to a discount on the eBook copy. Get in touch with us at service@packtpub.com for more details.

At www.PacktPub.com, you can also read a collection of free technical articles, sign up for a range of free newsletters and receive exclusive discounts and offers on Packt books and eBooks.

https://www2.packtpub.com/books/subscription/packtlib

Do you need instant solutions to your IT questions? PacktLib is Packt's online digital book library. Here, you can search, access, and read Packt's entire library of books.

Why subscribe?

- Fully searchable across every book published by Packt
- Copy and paste, print, and bookmark content
- On demand and accessible via a web browser

Free access for Packt account holders

If you have an account with Packt at www.PacktPub.com, you can use this to access PacktLib today and view 9 entirely free books. Simply use your login credentials for immediate access.

Table of Contents

Preface

LLVM is one of the very hot topics in recent times. It is an open source project with an ever-increasing number of contributors. Every programmer comes across a compiler at some point or the other while programming. Simply speaking, a compiler converts a high-level language to machine-executable code. However, what goes on under the hood is a lot of complex algorithms at work. So, to get started with compiler, LLVM will be the simplest infrastructure to study. Written in object-oriented C++, modular in design, and with concepts that are very easy to map to theory, LLVM proves to be attractive for experienced compiler programmers and for novice students who are willing to learn.

As authors, we maintain that simple solutions frequently work better and are easier to grasp than complex solutions. Throughout the book we will look at various topics that will help you enhance your skills and drive you to learn more.

We also believe that this book will be helpful for people not directly involved in compiler development as knowledge of compiler development will help them write code optimally.

What this book covers

Chapter 1, Playing with LLVM, introduces you to the modular design of LLVM and LLVM Intermediate Representation. In this chapter, we also look into some of the tools that LLVM provides.

Chapter 2, Building LLVM IR, introduces you to some basic function calls provided by the LLVM infrastructure to build LLVM IR. This chapter demonstrates building of modules, functions, basic blocks, condition statements, and loops using LLVM APIs.

Chapter 3, Advanced LLVM IR, introduces you to some advanced IR paradigms. This chapter explains advanced IR to the readers and shows how LLVM function calls can be used to emit them in the IR.

Chapter 4, Basic IR Transformations, deals with basic transformation optimizations at the IR level using the LLVM optimizer tool opt and the LLVM Pass infrastructure. You will learn how to use the information of one pass in another and then look into Instruction Simplification and Instruction Combining Passes.

Chapter 5, Advanced IR Block Transformations, deals with optimizations at block level on IR. We will discuss various optimizations such as Loop Optimizations, Scalar Evolution, Vectorization, and so on, followed by the summary of this chapter.

Chapter 6, IR to Selection DAG phase, takes you on a journey through the abstract infrastructure of a target-independent code generator. We explore how LLVM IR is converted to Selection DAG and various phases thereafter. It also introduces you to instruction selection, scheduling, register allocation, and so on.

Chapter 7, Generating Code for Target Architecture, introduces the readers to the tablegen concept. It shows how target architecture specifications such as register sets, instruction sets, calling conventions, and so on can be represented using tablegen, and how the output of tablegen can be used to emit code for a given architecture. This chapter can be used by readers as a reference for bootstrapping a target machine code generator.

What you need for this book

All you need to work through most of the examples covered in this book is a Linux machine, preferably Ubuntu. You will also need a simple text or code editor, Internet access, and a browser. We recommend installing the meld tool to compare two files; it works well on the Linux platform.

Who this book is for

This book is intended for those who already know some of the concepts concerning compilers and want to quickly become familiar with LLVM's infrastructure and the rich set of libraries that it provides. Compiler programmers, who are familiar with concepts of compilers and want to indulge in understanding, exploring, and using the LLVM infrastructure in a meaningful way in their work, will find this book useful.

This book is also for programmers who are not directly involved in compiler projects but are often involved in development phases where they write thousands of lines of code. With knowledge of how compilers work, they will be able to code in an optimal way and improve performance with clean code.

Conventions

In this book, you will find a number of text styles that distinguish between different kinds of information. Here are some examples of these styles and an explanation of their meaning.

Code words in text, database table names, folder names, filenames, file extensions, pathnames, dummy URLs, user input, and Twitter handles are shown as follows: "The LLVM `Pass Manager` uses the explicitly mentioned dependency information."

A block of code is set as follows:

```
int add(int a) {
return globvar + a;
}
```

When we wish to draw your attention to a particular part of a code block, the relevant lines or items are set in bold:

```
Value *StartVal = Builder.getInt32(1);
Value *Res = createLoop(Builder, List, VL, StartVal, Arg2);

Builder.CreateRet(Res);
```

Any command-line input or output is written as follows:

```
$ clang -emit-llvm -c -S add.c
$ cat add.ll
```

New terms and **important words** are shown in bold. Words that you see on the screen, for example, in menus or dialog boxes, appear in the text like this: "Clicking the **Next** button moves you to the next screen."

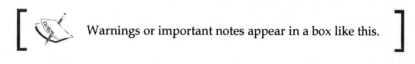

Warnings or important notes appear in a box like this.

Tips and tricks appear like this.

Reader feedback

Feedback from our readers is always welcome. Let us know what you think about this book—what you liked or disliked. Reader feedback is important for us as it helps us develop titles that you will really get the most out of.

To send us general feedback, simply e-mail feedback@packtpub.com, and mention the book's title in the subject of your message.

If there is a topic that you have expertise in and you are interested in either writing or contributing to a book, see our author guide at www.packtpub.com/authors.

Customer support

Now that you are the proud owner of a Packt book, we have a number of things to help you to get the most from your purchase.

Downloading the example code

You can download the example code files from your account at http://www.packtpub.com for all the Packt Publishing books you have purchased. If you purchased this book elsewhere, you can visit http://www.packtpub.com/support and register to have the files e-mailed directly to you.

Errata

Although we have taken every care to ensure the accuracy of our content, mistakes do happen. If you find a mistake in one of our books—maybe a mistake in the text or the code—we would be grateful if you could report this to us. By doing so, you can save other readers from frustration and help us improve subsequent versions of this book. If you find any errata, please report them by visiting http://www.packtpub.com/submit-errata, selecting your book, clicking on the **Errata Submission Form** link, and entering the details of your errata. Once your errata are verified, your submission will be accepted and the errata will be uploaded to our website or added to any list of existing errata under the Errata section of that title.

To view the previously submitted errata, go to https://www.packtpub.com/books/content/support and enter the name of the book in the search field. The required information will appear under the **Errata** section.

Piracy

Piracy of copyrighted material on the Internet is an ongoing problem across all media. At Packt, we take the protection of our copyright and licenses very seriously. If you come across any illegal copies of our works in any form on the Internet, please provide us with the location address or website name immediately so that we can pursue a remedy.

Please contact us at copyright@packtpub.com with a link to the suspected pirated material.

We appreciate your help in protecting our authors and our ability to bring you valuable content.

Questions

If you have a problem with any aspect of this book, you can contact us at questions@packtpub.com, and we will do our best to address the problem.

1
Playing with LLVM

The LLVM Compiler infrastructure project, started in 2000 in University of Illinois, was originally a research project to provide modern, SSA based compilation technique for arbitrary static and dynamic programming languages. Now it has grown to be an umbrella project with many sub projects within it, providing a set of reusable libraries having well defined interfaces.

LLVM is implemented in C++ and the main crux of it is the LLVM core libraries it provides. These libraries provide us with opt tool, the target independent optimizer, and code generation support for various target architectures. There are other tools which make use of core libraries, but our main focus in the book will be related to the three mentioned above. These are built around LLVM Intermediate Representation (LLVM IR), which can almost map all the high-level languages. So basically, to use LLVM's optimizer and code generation technique for code written in a certain programming language, all we need to do is write a frontend for a language that takes the high level language and generates LLVM IR. There are already many frontends available for languages such as C, C++, Go, Python, and so on. We will cover the following topics in this chapter:

- Modular design and collection of libraries
- Getting familiar with LLVM IR
- LLVM Tools and using them at command line

Modular design and collection of libraries

The most important thing about LLVM is that it is designed as a collection of libraries. Let's understand these by taking the example of LLVM optimizer opt. There are many different optimization passes that the optimizer can run. Each of these passes is written as a C++ class derived from the Pass class of LLVM. Each of the written passes can be compiled into a **.o** file and subsequently they are archived into a **.a** library. This library will contain all the passes for opt tool. All the passes in this library are loosely coupled, that is they mention explicitly the dependencies on other passes.

When the optimizer is ran, the LLVM PassManager uses the explicitly mentioned dependency information and runs the passes in optimal way. The library based design allows the implementer to choose the order in which passes will execute and also choose which passes are to be executed based on the requirements. Only the passes that are required are linked to the final application, not the entire optimizer.

The following figure demonstrates how each pass can be linked to a specific object file within a specific library. In the following figure, the **PassA** references **LLVMPasses.a** for **PassA.o**, whereas the custom pass refers to a different library **MyPasses.a** for the **MyPass.o** object file.

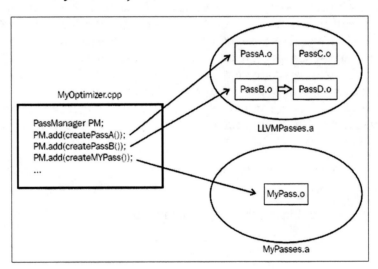

The code generator also makes use of this modular design like the **Optimizer**, for splitting the code generation into individual passes, namely, instruction selection, register allocation, scheduling, code layout optimization, and assembly emission.

In each of the following phases mentioned there are some common things for almost every target, such as an algorithm for assigning physical registers available to virtual registers even though the set of registers for different targets vary. So, the compiler writer can modify each of the passes mentioned above and create custom target-specific passes. The use of the `tablegen` tool helps in achieving this using table description `.td` files for specific architectures. We will discuss how this happens later in the book.

Another capability that arises out of this is the ability to easily pinpoint a bug to a particular pass in the optimizer. A tool name `Bugpoint` makes use of this capability to automatically reduce the test case and pinpoint the pass that is causing the bug.

Getting familiar with LLVM IR

LLVM **Intermediate Representation (IR)** is the heart of the LLVM project. In general every compiler produces an intermediate representation on which it runs most of its optimizations. For a compiler targeting multiple-source languages and different architectures the important decision while selecting an IR is that it should neither be of very high-level, as in very closely attached to the source language, nor it should be very low-level, as in close to the target machine instructions. LLVM IR aims to be a universal IR of a kind, by being at a low enough level that high-level ideas may be cleanly mapped to it. Ideally the LLVM IR should have been target-independent, but it is not so because of the inherent target dependence in some of the programming languages itself. For example, when using standard C headers in a Linux system, the header files itself are target dependent, which may specify a particular type to an entity so that it matches the system calls of the particular target architecture.

Most of the LLVM tools revolve around this Intermediate Representation. The frontends of different languages generate this IR from the high-level source language. The optimizer tool of LLVM runs on this generated IR to optimize the code for better performance and the code generator makes use of this IR for target specific code generation. This IR has three equivalent forms:

- An in-memory compiler IR
- An on-disk bitcode representation
- A Human readable form (LLVM Assembly)

Now let's take an example to see how this LLVM IR looks like. We will take a small C code and convert it into LLVM IR using clang and try to understand the details of LLVM IR by mapping it back to the source language.

```
$ cat add.c
int globvar = 12;

int add(int a) {
return globvar + a;
}
```

Use the clang frontend with the following options to convert it to LLVM IR:

```
$ clang -emit-llvm -c -S add.c
$ cat add.ll
; ModuleID = 'add.c'
target datalayout = "e-m:e-i64:64-f80:128-n8:16:32:64-S128"
target triple = "x86_64-unknown-linux-gnu"

@globvar = global i32 12, align 4

; Function Attrs: nounwind uwtable
define i32 @add(i32 %a) #0 {
  %1 = alloca i32, align 4
  store i32 %a, i32* %1, align 4
  %2 = load i32, i32* @globvar, align 4
  %3 = load i32, i32* %1, align 4
  %4 = add nsw i32 %2, %3
  ret i32 %4
}

attributes #0 = { nounwind uwtable "less-precise-fpmad"="false" "no-
frame-pointer-elim"="true" "no-frame-pointer-elim-non-leaf" "no-infs-fp-
math"="false" "no-nans-fp-math"="false" "stack-protector-buffer-size"="8"
"target-cpu"="x86-64" "unsafe-fp-math"="false" "use-soft-float"="false" }

!llvm.ident = !{!0}
```

Now let's look at the IR generated and see what it is all about. You can see the very first line giving the ModuleID, that it defines the LLVM module for add.c file. An LLVM module is a top–level data structure that has the entire contents of the input LLVM file. It consists of functions, global variables, external function prototypes, and symbol table entries.

The following lines show the target data layout and target triple from which we can know that the target is x86_64 processor with Linux running on it. The `datalayout` string tells us what is the endianess of machine ('e' meaning little endian), and the name mangling (`m : e` denotes elf type). Each specification is separated by '-'and each following spec gives information about the type and size of that type. For example, `i64:64` says 64 bit integer is of 64 bits.

Then we have a global variable `globvar`. In LLVM IR all globals start with '@' and all local variables start with '%'. There are two main reasons why the variables are prefixed with these symbols. The first one being, the compiler won't have to bother about a name clash with reserved words, the other being that the compiler can come up quickly with a temporary name without having to worry about a conflict with symbol table conflicts. This second property is useful for representing the IR in **static single assignment (SSA)** from where each variable is assigned only a single time and every use of a variable is preceded by its definition. So, while converting a normal program to SSA form, we create a new temporary name for every redefinition of a variable and limit the range of earlier definition till this redefinition.

LLVM views global variables as pointers, so an explicit dereference of the global variable using load instruction is required. Similarly, to store a value, an explicit store instruction is required.

Local variables have two categories:

- **Register allocated local variables**: These are the temporaries and allocated virtual registers. The virtual registers are allocated physical registers during the code generation phase which we will see in a later chapter of the book. They are created by using a new symbol for the variable like:

  ```
  %1 = some value
  ```

- **Stack allocated local variables**: These are created by allocating variables on the stack frame of a currently executing function, using the `alloca` instruction. The `alloca` instruction gives a pointer to the allocated type and explicit use of load and store instructions is required to access and store the value.

  ```
  %2 = alloca i32
  ```

Now let's see how the `add` function is represented in LLVM IR. `define i32 @add(i32 %a)` is very similar to how functions are declared in C. It specifies the function returns integer type `i32` and takes an integer argument. Also, the function name is preceded by '@', meaning it has global visibility.

Within the function is actual processing for functionality. Some important things to note here are that LLVM uses a three-address instruction, that is a data processing instruction, which has two source operands and places the result in a separate destination operand (%4 = add i32 %2, %3). Also the code is in SSA form, that is each value in the IR has a single assignment which defines the value. This is useful for a number of optimizations.

The attributes string that follows in the generated IR specifies the function attributes which are very similar to C++ attributes. These attributes are for the function that has been defined. For each function defined there is a set of attributes defined in the LLVM IR.

The code that follows the attributes is for the ident directive that identifies the module and compiler version.

LLVM tools and using them in the command line

Until now, we have understood what LLVM IR (human readable form) is and how it can be used to represent a high-level language. Now, we will take a look at some of the tools that LLVM provides so that we can play around with this IR converting to other formats and back again to the original form. Let's take a look at these tools one by one along with examples.

- **llvm-as**: This is the LLVM assembler that takes LLVM IR in assembly form (human readable) and converts it to bitcode format. Use the preceding add.ll as an example to convert it into bitcode. To know more about the LLVM Bitcode file format refer to http://llvm.org/docs/BitCodeFormat.html

  ```
  $ llvm-as add.ll -o add.bc
  ```

  To view the content of this bitcode file, a tool such as hexdump can be used.

  ```
  $ hexdump -c add.bc
  ```

- **llvm-dis**: This is the LLVM disassembler. It takes a bitcode file as input and outputs the llvm assembly.

  ```
  $ llvm-dis add.bc -o add.ll
  ```

  If you check add.ll and compare it with the previous version, it will be the same as the previous one.

- **llvm-link**: llvm-link links two or more llvm bitcode files and outputs one llvm bitcode file. To view a demo write a main.c file that calls the function in the add.c file.

```
$ cat main.c
#include<stdio.h>

extern int add(int);

int main() {
int a = add(2);
printf("%d\n",a);
return 0;
}
```

  Convert the C source code to LLVM bitcode format using the following command.

```
$ clang -emit-llvm -c main.c
```

  Now link main.bc and add.bc to generate output.bc.

```
$ llvm-link main.bc add.bc -o output.bc
```

- **lli**: lli directly executes programs in LLVM bitcode format using a just-in-time compiler or interpreter, if one is available for the current architecture. lli is not like a virtual machine and cannot execute IR of different architecture and can only interpret for host architecture. Use the bitcode format file generated by llvm-link as input to lli. It will display the output on the standard output.

```
$ lli output.bc
```

```
14
```

- **llc**: llc is the static compiler. It compiles LLVM inputs (assembly form/ bitcode form) into assembly language for a specified architecture. In the following example it takes the output.bc file generated by llvm-link and generates the assembly file output.s.

```
$ llc output.bc -o output.s
```

  Let's look at the content of the output.s assembly, specifically the two functions of the generated code, which is very similar to what a native assembler would have generated.

```
Function main:
   .type   main,@function
main:                                   # @main
   .cfi_startproc
# BB#0:
```

```
  pushq  %rbp
.Ltmp0:
  .cfi_def_cfa_offset 16
.Ltmp1:
  .cfi_offset %rbp, -16
  movq  %rsp, %rbp
.Ltmp2:
  .cfi_def_cfa_register %rbp
  subq  $16, %rsp
  movl  $0, -4(%rbp)
  movl  $2, %edi
  callq  add
  movl  %eax, %ecx
  movl  %ecx, -8(%rbp)
  movl  $.L.str, %edi
  xorl  %eax, %eax
  movl  %ecx, %esi
  callq  printf
  xorl  %eax, %eax
  addq  $16, %rsp
  popq  %rbp
  retq
.Lfunc_end0:


Function: add
add:                                    # @add
  .cfi_startproc
# BB#0:
  pushq  %rbp
.Ltmp3:
  .cfi_def_cfa_offset 16
.Ltmp4:
  .cfi_offset %rbp, -16
  movq  %rsp, %rbp
.Ltmp5:
  .cfi_def_cfa_register %rbp
  movl  %edi, -4(%rbp)
  addl  globvar(%rip), %edi
  movl  %edi, %eax
  popq  %rbp
  retq
.Lfunc_end1:
```

- **opt**: This is modular LLVM analyzer and optimizer. It takes the input file and runs the optimization or analysis specified on the command line. Whether it runs the analyzer or optimizer depends on the command-line option.

  ```
  opt [options] [input file name]
  ```

  When the `-analyze` option is provided it performs various analysis on the input. There is a set of analysis options already provided that can be specified through command line or else one can write down their own analysis pass and provide the library to that analysis pass. Some of the useful analysis passes that can be specified using the following command line arguments are:

  - **basicaa**: basic alias analysis
  - **da**: dependence analysis
  - **instcount**: count the various instruction types.
  - **loops**: information about loops
  - **scalar evolution**: analysis of scalar evolution

  When the `-analyze` option is not passed, the opt tool does the actual optimization work and tries to optimize the code depending upon the command-line options passed. Similarly to the preceding case, you can use some of the optimization passes already present or write your own pass for optimization. Some of the useful optimization passes that can be specified using the following command-line arguments are:

  - **constprop**: simple constant `propagation.`
  - **dce**: `dead` code elimination pass
  - **globalopt**: pass for global variable optimization
  - **inline**: pass for function inlining
  - **instcombine**: for combining redundant instructions
  - **licm**: loop invariant code motion
  - **tailcallelim**: Tail Call elimination

> Before going ahead we must note that all the tools mentioned in this chapter are meant for compiler writers. An end user can directly use clang for compilation of C code without converting the C code into intermediate representation

Summary

In this chapter, we looked into the modular design of LLVM: How it is used in the opt tool of LLVM, and how it is applicable across LLVM core libraries. Then we took a look into LLVM intermediate representation, and how various entities (variables, functions etc.) of a language are mapped to LLVM IR. In the last section, we discussed about some of the important LLVM tools, and how they can be used to transform the LLVM IR from one form to another.

In the next chapter, we will see how we can write a frontend for a language that can output LLVM IR using the LLVM machinery.

2

Building LLVM IR

A high level programming language facilitates human interaction with the target machine. Most of the popular high level languages today have certain basic elements such as variables, loops, if-else decision making statements, blocks, functions, and so on. A variable holds value of data types; a basic block gives an idea of the scope of the variable. An if-else decision statement helps in selection of a path of code. A function makes a block of code reusable. High level languages may vary in type checking, type casting, variable declarations, complex data types, and so on. However, almost every other language has the basic building blocks listed earlier in this section.

A language may have its own parser which tokenizes the statement and extracts meaningful information such as identifier, its data type; a function name, its declaration, definition and calls; a loop condition, and so on. This meaningful information may be stored in a data structure where the flow of the code can be easily retrieved. **Abstract Syntax Tree (AST)** is a popular tree representation of the source code. The AST's can be used for further transformation and analysis.

A language parser can be written in various ways with various tools such as lex, yacc, and so on, or can even be handwritten. Writing an efficient parser is an art in itself. But this is not what we intend to cover in this chapter. We would like to focus more on LLVM IR and how a high-level language after parsing can be converted to LLVM IR using LLVM libraries.

This chapter will cover how to construct basic working LLVM sample code, which includes the following:

- Creating an LLVM module
- Emitting a function in a module
- Adding a block to a function
- Emitting a global variable

- Emitting a return statement
- Emitting function arguments
- Emitting a simple arithmetic statement in a basic block
- Emitting if-else condition IR
- Emitting LLVM IR for loops

Creating an LLVM module

In the previous chapter, we got an idea as to how an LLVM IR looks. In LLVM, a module represents a single unit of code that is to be processed together. An LLVM module class is the top-level container for all other LLVM IR objects. The LLVM module contains global variables, functions, data layout, host triples, and so on. Let's create a simple LLVM module.

LLVM provides `Module()` constructor for creating a module. The first argument is the name of the module. The second argument is `LLVMContext`. Let's get these arguments in the main function and create a module as demonstrated here:

```
static LLVMContext &Context = getGlobalContext();
static Module *ModuleOb = new Module("my compiler", Context);
```

For these functions to work, we need to include certain header files:

```
#include "llvm/IR/LLVMContext.h"
#include "llvm/IR/Module.h"
using namespace llvm;
static LLVMContext &Context = getGlobalContext();
static Module *ModuleOb = new Module("my compiler", Context);

int main(int argc, char *argv[]) {
  ModuleOb->dump();
  return 0;
}
```

Put this code in a file, let's say `toy.cpp` and compile it:

```
$ clang++ -O3 toy.cpp `llvm-config --cxxflags --ldflags --system-libs
--libs core` -o toy
$ ./toy
```

The output will be as follows:

```
; ModuleID = 'my compiler'
```

Emitting a function in a module

Now that we have created a module, the next step is to emit a function. LLVM has an IRBuilder class that is used to generate LLVM IR and print it using the dump function of the Module object. LLVM provides the class llvm::Function to create a function and llvm::FunctionType() to associate a return type for the function. Let's assume that our foo() function returns an integer type.

```
Function *createFunc(IRBuilder<> &Builder, std::string Name) {
  FunctionType *funcType = llvm::FunctionType::get(Builder.
getInt32Ty(), false);
  Function *fooFunc = llvm::Function::Create(
      funcType, llvm::Function::ExternalLinkage, Name, ModuleOb);
  return fooFunc;
}
```

Finally, call function verifyFunction() on fooFunc. This function performs a variety of consistency checks on the generated code, to determine if our compiler is doing everything right.

```
int main(int argc, char *argv[]) {
  static IRBuilder<> Builder(Context);
  Function *fooFunc = createFunc(Builder, "foo");
  verifyFunction(*fooFunc);
  ModuleOb->dump();
  return 0;
}
```

Add the IR/IRBuilder.h, IR/DerivedTypes.h and IR/Verifier.h file in include section.

The overall code is as follows:

```
#include "llvm/IR/IRBuilder.h"
#include "llvm/IR/LLVMContext.h"
#include "llvm/IR/Module.h"
#include "llvm/IR/Verifier.h"
#include <vector>
using namespace llvm;

static LLVMContext &Context = getGlobalContext();
static Module *ModuleOb = new Module("my compiler", Context);

Function *createFunc(IRBuilder<> &Builder, std::string Name) {
  FunctionType *funcType = llvm::FunctionType::get(Builder.
getInt32Ty(), false);
```

```
    Function *fooFunc = llvm::Function::Create(
        funcType, llvm::Function::ExternalLinkage, Name, ModuleOb);
    return fooFunc;
}

int main(int argc, char *argv[]) {
    static IRBuilder<> Builder(Context);
    Function *fooFunc = createFunc(Builder, "foo");
    verifyFunction(*fooFunc);
    ModuleOb->dump();
    return 0;
}
```

Compile the toy.cpp with the same options as stated earlier

```
$ clang++ -O3 toy.cpp `llvm-config --cxxflags --ldflags --system-libs
--libs core` -o toy
```

The output will be as follows:

```
$ ./toy
; ModuleID = 'my compiler'


declare i32 @foo()
```

Adding a block to a function

A function consists of basic blocks. A basic block has an entry point. A basic block consists of a number of IR instructions, the last instruction being a terminator instruction. It has single exit point. LLVM provides the BasicBlock class to create and handle basic blocks. A basic block might have an entry point as its label, which indicates where to insert the next instructions. We can use the IRBuilder object to hold these new basic block IR.

```
BasicBlock *createBB(Function *fooFunc, std::string Name) {
    return BasicBlock::Create(Context, Name, fooFunc);
}
```

The overall code is as follows:

```
#include "llvm/IR/IRBuilder.h"
#include "llvm/IR/LLVMContext.h"
#include "llvm/IR/Module.h"
```

```cpp
#include "llvm/IR/Verifier.h"
#include <vector>
using namespace llvm;

static LLVMContext &Context = getGlobalContext();
static Module *ModuleOb = new Module("my compiler", Context);

Function *createFunc(IRBuilder<> &Builder, std::string Name) {
  FunctionType *funcType = llvm::FunctionType::get(Builder.
  getInt32Ty(), false);
  Function *fooFunc = llvm::Function::Create(
      funcType, llvm::Function::ExternalLinkage, Name, ModuleOb);
  return fooFunc;
}

BasicBlock *createBB(Function *fooFunc, std::string Name) {
  return BasicBlock::Create(Context, Name, fooFunc);
}

int main(int argc, char *argv[]) {
  static IRBuilder<> Builder(Context);
  Function *fooFunc = createFunc(Builder, "foo");
  BasicBlock *entry = createBB(fooFunc, "entry");
  Builder.SetInsertPoint(entry);
  verifyFunction(*fooFunc);
  ModuleOb->dump();
  return 0;
}
```

Compile the `toy.cpp` file:

```
$ clang++ -O3 toy.cpp `llvm-config --cxxflags --ldflags --system-libs
--libs core` -o toy
```

The output will be as follows:

```
; ModuleID = 'my compiler'

define i32 @foo() {
entry:
}
```

Emitting a global variable

Global variables have visibility of all the functions within a given module. LLVM provides the `GlobalVariable` class to create global variables and set its properties such as linkage type, alignment, and so on. The `Module` class has the method `getOrInsertGlobal()` to create a global variable. It takes two arguments — the first is the name of the variable and the second is the data type of the variable.

As global variables are part of a module, we create global variables after creating the module. Insert the following code just after creating the module in `toy.cpp`:

```
GlobalVariable *createGlob(IRBuilder<> &Builder, std::string Name) {
    ModuleOb->getOrInsertGlobal(Name, Builder.getInt32Ty());
    GlobalVariable *gVar = ModuleOb->getNamedGlobal(Name);
    gVar->setLinkage(GlobalValue::CommonLinkage);
    gVar->setAlignment(4);
    return gVar;
}
```

Linkage is what determines if multiple declarations of the same object refer to the same object, or to separate ones. The LLVM reference manual cites the following types of Linkages:

`ExternalLinkage`	Externally visible function.
`AvailableExternallyLinkage`	Available for inspection, not emission.
`LinkOnceAnyLinkage`	Keep one copy of function when linking (inline)
`LinkOnceODRLinkage`	Same, but only replaced by something equivalent.
`WeakAnyLinkage`	Keep one copy of named function when linking (weak)
`WeakODRLinkage`	Same, but only replaced by something equivalent.
`AppendingLinkage`	Special purpose, only applies to global arrays.
`InternalLinkage`	Rename collisions when linking (static functions).
`PrivateLinkage`	Like internal, but omit from symbol table.
`ExternalWeakLinkage`	`ExternalWeak` linkage description.
`CommonLinkage`	Tentative definitions

Alignment gives information about address alignment. An alignment must be a power of 2. If not specified explicitly, it is set by the target. The maximum alignment is `1 << 29`.

The overall code is as follows:

```
#include "llvm/IR/IRBuilder.h"
#include "llvm/IR/LLVMContext.h"
#include "llvm/IR/Module.h"
#include "llvm/IR/Verifier.h"
#include <vector>
using namespace llvm;

static LLVMContext &Context = getGlobalContext();
static Module *ModuleOb = new Module("my compiler", Context);

Function *createFunc(IRBuilder<> &Builder, std::string Name) {
  FunctionType *funcType = llvm::FunctionType::get(Builder.
getInt32Ty(), false);
  Function *fooFunc = llvm::Function::Create(
      funcType, llvm::Function::ExternalLinkage, Name, ModuleOb);
  return fooFunc;
}

BasicBlock *createBB(Function *fooFunc, std::string Name) {
  return BasicBlock::Create(Context, Name, fooFunc);
}

GlobalVariable *createGlob(IRBuilder<> &Builder, std::string Name) {
  ModuleOb->getOrInsertGlobal(Name, Builder.getInt32Ty());
  GlobalVariable *gVar = ModuleOb->getNamedGlobal(Name);
  gVar->setLinkage(GlobalValue::CommonLinkage);
  gVar->setAlignment(4);
  return gVar;
}

int main(int argc, char *argv[]) {
  static IRBuilder<> Builder(Context);
  GlobalVariable *gVar = createGlob(Builder, "x");
  Function *fooFunc = createFunc(Builder, "foo");
  BasicBlock *entry = createBB(fooFunc, "entry");
  Builder.SetInsertPoint(entry);
  verifyFunction(*fooFunc);
  ModuleOb->dump();
  return 0;
}
```

Compile the `toy.cpp`

```
$ clang++ -O3 toy.cpp `llvm-config --cxxflags --ldflags --system-libs
--libs core` -o toy
```

The output will be as follows:

```
; ModuleID = 'my compiler'

@x = common global i32, align 4

define i32 @foo() {
entry:
}
```

Emitting a return statement

A function might return a value or it may return void. Here in our example, we have defined that our function returns an integer. Let's assume that our function returns 0. The first step is to get a 0 value, which can be done using the `Constant` class.

```
Builder.CreateRet(Builder.getInt32(0));
```

The overall code is as follows:

```
#include "llvm/IR/IRBuilder.h"
#include "llvm/IR/LLVMContext.h"
#include "llvm/IR/Module.h"
#include "llvm/IR/Verifier.h"
#include <vector>
using namespace llvm;

static LLVMContext &Context = getGlobalContext();
static Module *ModuleOb = new Module("my compiler", Context);

Function *createFunc(IRBuilder<> &Builder, std::string Name) {
  FunctionType *funcType = llvm::FunctionType::get(Builder.
  getInt32Ty(), false);
  Function *fooFunc = llvm::Function::Create(
      funcType, llvm::Function::ExternalLinkage, Name, ModuleOb);
  return fooFunc;
```

```
  }

  BasicBlock *createBB(Function *fooFunc, std::string Name) {
    return BasicBlock::Create(Context, Name, fooFunc);
  }

  GlobalVariable *createGlob(IRBuilder<> &Builder, std::string Name) {
    ModuleOb->getOrInsertGlobal(Name, Builder.getInt32Ty());
    GlobalVariable *gVar = ModuleOb->getNamedGlobal(Name);
    gVar->setLinkage(GlobalValue::CommonLinkage);
    gVar->setAlignment(4);
    return gVar;
  }

  int main(int argc, char *argv[]) {
    static IRBuilder<> Builder(Context);
    GlobalVariable *gVar = createGlob(Builder, "x");
    Function *fooFunc = createFunc(Builder, "foo");
    BasicBlock *entry = createBB(fooFunc, "entry");
    Builder.SetInsertPoint(entry);
    Builder.CreateRet(Builder.getInt32(0));
    verifyFunction(*fooFunc);
    ModuleOb->dump();
    return 0;
  }
```

Compile `toy.cpp` file

```
$ clang++ -O3 toy.cpp `llvm-config --cxxflags --ldflags --system-libs
--libs core` -o toy
```

The output will be as follows:

```
  ; ModuleID = 'my compiler'

  @x = common global i32, align 4

  define i32 @foo() {
  entry:
    ret i32 0
  }
```

Emitting function arguments

A function takes arguments that have their own data type. For simplification, assume that our function has all the arguments of i32 type (integer 32 bit).

For example, we will consider that two arguments, a and b, are passed to the function. We will store these two arguments in a vector:

```
static std::vector<std::string> FunArgs;
FunArgs.push_back("a");
FunArgs.push_back("b");
```

The next step is to specify that the function will have two arguments. This can be done by passing the Integer argument to the functiontype.

```
Function *createFunc(IRBuilder<> &Builder, std::string Name) {
  std::vector<Type *> Integers(FunArgs.size(),
Type::getInt32Ty(Context));
  FunctionType *funcType =
      llvm::FunctionType::get(Builder.getInt32Ty(), Integers, false);
  Function *fooFunc = llvm::Function::Create(
      funcType, llvm::Function::ExternalLinkage, Name, ModuleOb);
  return fooFunc;
}
```

The last step is to set the names of the function arguments. This can be done by Function argument iterator in a loop, as shown:

```
void setFuncArgs(Function *fooFunc, std::vector<std::string> FunArgs)
{
  unsigned Idx = 0;
  Function::arg_iterator AI, AE;
  for (AI = fooFunc->arg_begin(), AE = fooFunc->arg_end(); AI != AE;
      ++AI, ++Idx)
    AI->setName(FunArgs[Idx]);
}
```

The overall code is as follows:

```
#include "llvm/IR/IRBuilder.h"
#include "llvm/IR/LLVMContext.h"
#include "llvm/IR/Module.h"
#include "llvm/IR/Verifier.h"
#include <vector>
```

```
using namespace llvm;

static LLVMContext &Context = getGlobalContext();
static Module *ModuleOb = new Module("my compiler", Context);
static std::vector<std::string> FunArgs;

Function *createFunc(IRBuilder<> &Builder, std::string Name) {
  std::vector<Type *> Integers(FunArgs.size(),
Type::getInt32Ty(Context));
  FunctionType *funcType =
      llvm::FunctionType::get(Builder.getInt32Ty(), Integers, false);
  Function *fooFunc = llvm::Function::Create(
      funcType, llvm::Function::ExternalLinkage, Name, ModuleOb);
  return fooFunc;
}


void setFuncArgs(Function *fooFunc, std::vector<std::string> FunArgs)
{
  unsigned Idx = 0;
  Function::arg_iterator AI, AE;
  for (AI = fooFunc->arg_begin(), AE = fooFunc->arg_end(); AI != AE;
       ++AI, ++Idx)
    AI->setName(FunArgs[Idx]);
}

BasicBlock *createBB(Function *fooFunc, std::string Name) {
  return BasicBlock::Create(Context, Name, fooFunc);
}

GlobalVariable *createGlob(IRBuilder<> &Builder, std::string Name) {
  ModuleOb->getOrInsertGlobal(Name, Builder.getInt32Ty());
  GlobalVariable *gVar = ModuleOb->getNamedGlobal(Name);
  gVar->setLinkage(GlobalValue::CommonLinkage);
  gVar->setAlignment(4);
  return gVar;
}

int main(int argc, char *argv[]) {
  FunArgs.push_back("a");
  FunArgs.push_back("b");
  static IRBuilder<> Builder(Context);
  GlobalVariable *gVar = createGlob(Builder, "x");
  Function *fooFunc = createFunc(Builder, "foo");
```

```
    setFuncArgs(fooFunc, FunArgs);
    BasicBlock *entry = createBB(fooFunc, "entry");
    Builder.SetInsertPoint(entry);
    Builder.CreateRet(Builder.getInt32(0));
    verifyFunction(*fooFunc);
    ModuleOb->dump();
    return 0;
}
```

Compile the `toy.cpp` file:

```
$ clang++ -O3 toy.cpp `llvm-config --cxxflags --ldflags --system-libs
--libs core` -o toy
```

The output will be as follows:

```
; ModuleID = 'my compiler'

@x = common global i32, align 4

define i32 @foo(i32 %a, i32 %b) {
entry:
  ret i32 0
}
```

Emitting a simple arithmetic statement in a basic block

A basic block consists of a list of instructions. For example, an instruction can be a simple statement performing tasks based on some simple arithmetic instruction. We will see how the LLVM API can be used to emit arithmetic instructions.

For example, if we want to multiply first argument a with integer value 16, we will create a constant integer value 16 with the following API:

```
Value *constant = Builder.getInt32(16);
```

We already have a from the function argument list:

```
Value *Arg1 = fooFunc->arg_begin();
```

LLVM provides a rich list of API's to create binary operations. You can go through the include/llvm/IR/IRBuild.h file for more details on the APIs.

```
Value *createArith(IRBuilder<> &Builder, Value *L, Value *R) {
  return Builder.CreateMul(L, R, "multmp");
}
```

 Note that for demo purposes, the preceding function returns multiplication. We leave it to the readers to make this function more flexible to return any binary operations. You can explore more binary operations in include/llvm/IR/IRBuild.h.

The whole code now looks as follows:

```
#include "llvm/IR/IRBuilder.h"
#include "llvm/IR/LLVMContext.h"
#include "llvm/IR/Module.h"
#include "llvm/IR/Verifier.h"
#include <vector>
using namespace llvm;

static LLVMContext &Context = getGlobalContext();
static Module *ModuleOb = new Module("my compiler", Context);
static std::vector<std::string> FunArgs;

Function *createFunc(IRBuilder<> &Builder, std::string Name) {
  std::vector<Type *> Integers(FunArgs.size(),
  Type::getInt32Ty(Context));
  FunctionType *funcType =
      llvm::FunctionType::get(Builder.getInt32Ty(), Integers, false);
  Function *fooFunc = llvm::Function::Create(
      funcType, llvm::Function::ExternalLinkage, Name, ModuleOb);
  return fooFunc;
}

void setFuncArgs(Function *fooFunc, std::vector<std::string> FunArgs)
{

  unsigned Idx = 0;
  Function::arg_iterator AI, AE;
```

```
  for (AI = fooFunc->arg_begin(), AE = fooFunc->arg_end(); AI != AE;
       ++AI, ++Idx)
    AI->setName(FunArgs[Idx]);
}

BasicBlock *createBB(Function *fooFunc, std::string Name) {
  return BasicBlock::Create(Context, Name, fooFunc);
}

GlobalVariable *createGlob(IRBuilder<> &Builder, std::string Name) {
  ModuleOb->getOrInsertGlobal(Name, Builder.getInt32Ty());
  GlobalVariable *gVar = ModuleOb->getNamedGlobal(Name);
  gVar->setLinkage(GlobalValue::CommonLinkage);
  gVar->setAlignment(4);
  return gVar;
}

Value *createArith(IRBuilder<> &Builder, Value *L, Value *R) {
  return Builder.CreateMul(L, R, "multmp");
}

int main(int argc, char *argv[]) {
  FunArgs.push_back("a");
  FunArgs.push_back("b");
  static IRBuilder<> Builder(Context);
  GlobalVariable *gVar = createGlob(Builder, "x");
  Function *fooFunc = createFunc(Builder, "foo");
  setFuncArgs(fooFunc, FunArgs);
  BasicBlock *entry = createBB(fooFunc, "entry");
  Builder.SetInsertPoint(entry);
  Value *Arg1 = fooFunc->arg_begin();
  Value *constant = Builder.getInt32(16);
  Value *val = createArith(Builder, Arg1, constant);
  Builder.CreateRet(val);
  verifyFunction(*fooFunc);
  ModuleOb->dump();
  return 0;
}
```

Compile the following program:

```
$ clang++ -O3 toy.cpp `llvm-config --cxxflags --ldflags
--system-libs --libs core` -o toy
```

The output will be as follows:

```
; ModuleID = 'my compiler'

@x = common global i32, align 4

define i32 @foo(i32 %a, i32 %b) {
entry:
  %multmp = mul i32 %a, 16
  ret i32 %multmp
}
```

Did you notice the return value? We returned the multiplication instead of constant 0.

Emitting if-else condition IR

An **if-else** statement has a condition expression and two code paths to execute, depending on the condition evaluating to true or false. The condition expression is generally a comparison statement. Let's emit a condition statement at the start of the block. For example, let the condition be like a<100.

```
Value *val2 = Builder.getInt32(100);
Value *Compare = Builder.CreateICmpULT(val, val2, "cmptmp");
```

On compilation, we get following output:

```
; ModuleID = 'my compiler'

@x = common global i32, align 4

define i32 @foo(i32 %a, i32 %b) {
entry:
  %multmp = mul i32 %a, 16
  %cmptmp = icmp ult i32 %multmp, 100

  ret i32 %multmp
}
```

The next step is to define the then and else block expressions, which will be executed depending on the result of condition expression "booltmp". Here, an important concept of **PHI** instruction comes into picture. A phi instruction takes various values coming from different basic blocks and decides which value to assign depending on the condition expression.

Two separate basic blocks "ThenBB" and "ElseBB" will be created. Let's say that the then expression is 'add 1 to a' and else expression is 'add 2 to a'.

A third block will represent the merge block, which contains the instructions to be executed at the merging of the then and else blocks. These blocks need to be pushed into the function foo().

For reusability, we create BasicBlock and Value containers as follows:

```
typedef SmallVector<BasicBlock *, 16> BBList;
typedef SmallVector<Value *, 16> ValList;
```

 Note that SmallVector<> is vector container wrapper provided by LLVM for simplicity.

We also push some of the values in a Value* list to process them in the if-else block, as follows:

```
Value *Condtn = Builder.CreateICmpNE(Compare, Builder.getInt32(0),
"ifcond");
ValList VL;
VL.push_back(Condtn);
VL.push_back(Arg1);
```

We create three basic blocks and push them in container, as follows:

```
BasicBlock *ThenBB = createBB(fooFunc, "then");
BasicBlock *ElseBB = createBB(fooFunc, "else");
BasicBlock *MergeBB = createBB(fooFunc, "ifcont");
BBList List;
List.push_back(ThenBB);
List.push_back(ElseBB);
List.push_back(MergeBB);
```

We finally create a function to emit the if-else block:

```
Value *createIfElse(IRBuilder<> &Builder, BBList List, ValList VL) {
  Value *Condtn = VL[0];
  Value *Arg1 = VL[1];
  BasicBlock *ThenBB = List[0];
  BasicBlock *ElseBB = List[1];
  BasicBlock *MergeBB = List[2];
  Builder.CreateCondBr(Condtn, ThenBB, ElseBB);

  Builder.SetInsertPoint(ThenBB);
```

```
   Value *ThenVal = Builder.CreateAdd(Arg1, Builder.getInt32(1),
"thenaddtmp");
   Builder.CreateBr(MergeBB);

   Builder.SetInsertPoint(ElseBB);
   Value *ElseVal = Builder.CreateAdd(Arg1, Builder.getInt32(2),
"elseaddtmp");
   Builder.CreateBr(MergeBB);

   unsigned PhiBBSize = List.size() - 1;
   Builder.SetInsertPoint(MergeBB);
   PHINode *Phi = Builder.CreatePHI(Type::getInt32Ty(getGlobalConte
xt()), PhiBBSize, "iftmp");
   Phi->addIncoming(ThenVal, ThenBB);
   Phi->addIncoming(ElseVal, ElseBB);

   return Phi;
}
```

Overall code:

```
#include "llvm/IR/IRBuilder.h"
#include "llvm/IR/LLVMContext.h"
#include "llvm/IR/Module.h"
#include "llvm/IR/Verifier.h"
#include <vector>
using namespace llvm;

static LLVMContext &Context = getGlobalContext();
static Module *ModuleOb = new Module("my compiler", Context);
static std::vector<std::string> FunArgs;
typedef SmallVector<BasicBlock *, 16> BBList;
typedef SmallVector<Value *, 16> ValList;

Function *createFunc(IRBuilder<> &Builder, std::string Name) {
  std::vector<Type *> Integers(FunArgs.size(),
Type::getInt32Ty(Context));
  FunctionType *funcType =
      llvm::FunctionType::get(Builder.getInt32Ty(), Integers, false);
  Function *fooFunc = llvm::Function::Create(
      funcType, llvm::Function::ExternalLinkage, Name, ModuleOb);
  return fooFunc;
```

```
    }

    void setFuncArgs(Function *fooFunc, std::vector<std::string> FunArgs)
    {

      unsigned Idx = 0;
      Function::arg_iterator AI, AE;
      for (AI = fooFunc->arg_begin(), AE = fooFunc->arg_end(); AI != AE;
           ++AI, ++Idx)
        AI->setName(FunArgs[Idx]);
    }

    BasicBlock *createBB(Function *fooFunc, std::string Name) {
      return BasicBlock::Create(Context, Name, fooFunc);
    }

    GlobalVariable *createGlob(IRBuilder<> &Builder, std::string Name) {
      ModuleOb->getOrInsertGlobal(Name, Builder.getInt32Ty());
      GlobalVariable *gVar = ModuleOb->getNamedGlobal(Name);
      gVar->setLinkage(GlobalValue::CommonLinkage);
      gVar->setAlignment(4);
      return gVar;
    }

    Value *createArith(IRBuilder<> &Builder, Value *L, Value *R) {
      return Builder.CreateMul(L, R, "multmp");
    }

    Value *createIfElse(IRBuilder<> &Builder, BBList List, ValList VL) {
      Value *Condtn = VL[0];
      Value *Arg1 = VL[1];
      BasicBlock *ThenBB = List[0];
      BasicBlock *ElseBB = List[1];
      BasicBlock *MergeBB = List[2];
      Builder.CreateCondBr(Condtn, ThenBB, ElseBB);

      Builder.SetInsertPoint(ThenBB);
      Value *ThenVal = Builder.CreateAdd(Arg1, Builder.getInt32(1),
    "thenaddtmp");
      Builder.CreateBr(MergeBB);

      Builder.SetInsertPoint(ElseBB);
```

```
   Value *ElseVal = Builder.CreateAdd(Arg1, Builder.getInt32(2),
   "elseaddtmp");
   Builder.CreateBr(MergeBB);

   unsigned PhiBBSize = List.size() - 1;
   Builder.SetInsertPoint(MergeBB);
   PHINode *Phi = Builder.CreatePHI(Type::getInt32Ty(getGlobalConte
   xt()), PhiBBSize, "iftmp");
   PhiBBSize, "iftmp");
   Phi->addIncoming(ThenVal, ThenBB);
   Phi->addIncoming(ElseVal, ElseBB);

   return Phi;
}

int main(int argc, char *argv[]) {
  FunArgs.push_back("a");
  FunArgs.push_back("b");
  static IRBuilder<> Builder(Context);
  GlobalVariable *gVar = createGlob(Builder, "x");
  Function *fooFunc = createFunc(Builder, "foo");
  setFuncArgs(fooFunc, FunArgs);
  BasicBlock *entry = createBB(fooFunc, "entry");
  Builder.SetInsertPoint(entry);
  Value *Arg1 = fooFunc->arg_begin();
  Value *constant = Builder.getInt32(16);
  Value *val = createArith(Builder, Arg1, constant);

  Value *val2 = Builder.getInt32(100);
  Value *Compare = Builder.CreateICmpULT(val, val2, "cmptmp");
  Value *Condtn = Builder.CreateICmpNE(Compare, Builder.getInt32(0),
  "ifcond");

  ValList VL;
  VL.push_back(Condtn);
  VL.push_back(Arg1);

  BasicBlock *ThenBB = createBB(fooFunc, "then");
  BasicBlock *ElseBB = createBB(fooFunc, "else");
  BasicBlock *MergeBB = createBB(fooFunc, "ifcont");
  BBList List;
  List.push_back(ThenBB);
  List.push_back(ElseBB);
```

```
    List.push_back(MergeBB);

    Value *v = createIfElse(Builder, List, VL);

    Builder.CreateRet(v);
    verifyFunction(*fooFunc);
    ModuleOb->dump();
    return 0;
}
```

After compiling, the output looks like the following:

```
; ModuleID = 'my compiler'

@x = common global i32, align 4

define i32 @foo(i32 %a, i32 %b) {
entry:
  %multmp = mul i32 %a, 16
  %cmptmp = icmp ult i32 %multmp, 100
  %ifcond = icmp ne i1 %cmptmp, i32 0
  br i1 %ifcond, label %then, label %else

then:                                            ; preds = %entry
  %thenaddtmp = add i32 %a, 1
  br label %ifcont

else:                                            ; preds = %entry
  %elseaddtmp = add i32 %a, 2
  br label %ifcont

ifcont:                                          ; preds = %else,
%then
  %iftmp = phi i32 [ %thenaddtmp, %then ], [ %elseaddtmp, %else ]
  ret i32 %iftmp
}
```

Emitting LLVM IR for loop

Similar to the if-else statement, loops can also be emitted using LLVM API's, with slight modification of the code. For example, we want to have LLVM IR for the following Loops:

```
for(i=1; i< b; i++)  {body}
```

The loop has induction variable i, which has some initial value that updates after each iteration. The induction variable is updated after each iteration by a step value that is 1 in the preceding example. Then there is a loop ending condition. In the preceding example, 'i=1' is the initial value, 'i<b' is the end condition of the loop, and 'i++' is the step value by which the induction variable 'i' is incremented after every iteration of the loop.

Before writing a function to create a loop, some Value and BasicBlock need to be pushed into a list, as follows:

```
Function::arg_iterator AI = fooFunc->arg_begin();
  Value *Arg1 = AI++;
  Value *Arg2 = AI;
  Value *constant = Builder.getInt32(16);
  Value *val = createArith(Builder, Arg1, constant);
  ValList VL;
  VL.push_back(Arg1);

  BBList List;
  BasicBlock *LoopBB = createBB(fooFunc, "loop");
  BasicBlock *AfterBB = createBB(fooFunc, "afterloop");
  List.push_back(LoopBB);
  List.push_back(AfterBB);

  Value *StartVal = Builder.getInt32(1);
```

Let's create a function for the emitting loop:

```
PHINode *createLoop(IRBuilder<> &Builder, BBList List, ValList VL,
                    Value *StartVal, Value *EndVal) {
  BasicBlock *PreheaderBB = Builder.GetInsertBlock();
  Value *val = VL[0];
  BasicBlock *LoopBB = List[0];
  Builder.CreateBr(LoopBB);
  Builder.SetInsertPoint(LoopBB);
  PHINode *IndVar = Builder.CreatePHI(Type::getInt32Ty(Context), 2,
  "i");
  IndVar->addIncoming(StartVal, PreheaderBB);
  Builder.CreateAdd(val, Builder.getInt32(5), "addtmp");
  Value *StepVal = Builder.getInt32(1);
  Value *NextVal = Builder.CreateAdd(IndVar, StepVal, "nextval");
  Value *EndCond = Builder.CreateICmpULT(IndVar, EndVal, "endcond");
  EndCond = Builder.CreateICmpNE(EndCond, Builder.getInt32(0),
  "loopcond");
```

```
   BasicBlock *LoopEndBB = Builder.GetInsertBlock();
   BasicBlock *AfterBB = List[1];
   Builder.CreateCondBr(EndCond, LoopBB, AfterBB);
   Builder.SetInsertPoint(AfterBB);
   IndVar->addIncoming(NextVal, LoopEndBB);
   return IndVar;
}
```

Consider the following lines of code:

```
IndVar->addIncoming(StartVal, PreheaderBB);...
IndVar->addIncoming(NextVal, LoopEndBB);
```

IndVar is a PHI node, which has two incoming values from two blocks — startval from the Preheader block (i=1), and Nextval from the LoopEnd block.

The overall code is as follows:

```
#include "llvm/IR/IRBuilder.h"
#include "llvm/IR/LLVMContext.h"
#include "llvm/IR/Module.h"
#include "llvm/IR/Verifier.h"
#include <vector>
using namespace llvm;

typedef SmallVector<BasicBlock *, 16> BBList;
typedef SmallVector<Value *, 16> ValList;

static LLVMContext &Context = getGlobalContext();
static Module *ModuleOb = new Module("my compiler", Context);
static std::vector<std::string> FunArgs;

Function *createFunc(IRBuilder<> &Builder, std::string Name) {
  std::vector<Type *> Integers(FunArgs.size(),
  Type::getInt32Ty(Context));
  FunctionType *funcType =
      llvm::FunctionType::get(Builder.getInt32Ty(), Integers, false);
  Function *fooFunc = llvm::Function::Create(
      funcType, llvm::Function::ExternalLinkage, Name, ModuleOb);
  return fooFunc;
}

void setFuncArgs(Function *fooFunc, std::vector<std::string> FunArgs)
{

  unsigned Idx = 0;
```

```
    Function::arg_iterator AI, AE;
    for (AI = fooFunc->arg_begin(), AE = fooFunc->arg_end(); AI != AE;
         ++AI, ++Idx)
      AI->setName(FunArgs[Idx]);
  }


BasicBlock *createBB(Function *fooFunc, std::string Name) {
    return BasicBlock::Create(Context, Name, fooFunc);
  }


GlobalVariable *createGlob(IRBuilder<> &Builder, std::string Name) {
    ModuleOb->getOrInsertGlobal(Name, Builder.getInt32Ty());
    GlobalVariable *gVar = ModuleOb->getNamedGlobal(Name);
    gVar->setLinkage(GlobalValue::CommonLinkage);
    gVar->setAlignment(4);
    return gVar;
  }


Value *createArith(IRBuilder<> &Builder, Value *L, Value *R) {
    return Builder.CreateMul(L, R, "multmp");
  }


Value *createLoop(IRBuilder<> &Builder, BBList List, ValList VL,
                    Value *StartVal, Value *EndVal) {
  BasicBlock *PreheaderBB = Builder.GetInsertBlock();
  Value *val = VL[0];
  BasicBlock *LoopBB = List[0];
  Builder.CreateBr(LoopBB);
  Builder.SetInsertPoint(LoopBB);
  PHINode *IndVar = Builder.CreatePHI(Type::getInt32Ty(Context), 2,
"i");
  IndVar->addIncoming(StartVal, PreheaderBB);
  Value *Add = Builder.CreateAdd(val, Builder.getInt32(5), "addtmp");
  Value *StepVal = Builder.getInt32(1);
  Value *NextVal = Builder.CreateAdd(IndVar, StepVal, "nextval");
  Value *EndCond = Builder.CreateICmpULT(IndVar, EndVal, "endcond");
  EndCond = Builder.CreateICmpNE(EndCond, Builder.getInt32(0),
"loopcond");
  BasicBlock *LoopEndBB = Builder.GetInsertBlock();
  BasicBlock *AfterBB = List[1];
  Builder.CreateCondBr(EndCond, LoopBB, AfterBB);
  Builder.SetInsertPoint(AfterBB);
  IndVar->addIncoming(NextVal, LoopEndBB);
  return Add;
```

```
    }

    int main(int argc, char *argv[]) {
      FunArgs.push_back("a");
      FunArgs.push_back("b");
      static IRBuilder<> Builder(Context);
      GlobalVariable *gVar = createGlob(Builder, "x");
      Function *fooFunc = createFunc(Builder, "foo");
      setFuncArgs(fooFunc, FunArgs);
      BasicBlock *entry = createBB(fooFunc, "entry");
      Builder.SetInsertPoint(entry);
      Function::arg_iterator AI = fooFunc->arg_begin();
      Value *Arg1 = AI++;
      Value *Arg2 = AI;
      Value *constant = Builder.getInt32(16);
      Value *val = createArith(Builder, Arg1, constant);
      ValList VL;
      VL.push_back(Arg1);

      BBList List;
      BasicBlock *LoopBB = createBB(fooFunc, "loop");
      BasicBlock *AfterBB = createBB(fooFunc, "afterloop");
      List.push_back(LoopBB);
      List.push_back(AfterBB);

      Value *StartVal = Builder.getInt32(1);
      Value *Res = createLoop(Builder, List, VL, StartVal, Arg2);

      Builder.CreateRet(Res);
      verifyFunction(*fooFunc);
      ModuleOb->dump();
      return 0;
    }
```

After compiling the program, we get the following output:

```
; ModuleID = 'my compiler'

@x = common global i32, align 4

define i32 @foo(i32 %a, i32 %b) {
entry:
  %multmp = mul i32 %a, 16
```

```
    br label %loop

  loop:                                              ; preds = %loop,
  %entry
    %i = phi i32 [ 1, %entry ], [ %nextval, %loop ]
    %addtmp = add i32 %a, 5
    %nextval = add i32 %i, 1
    %endcond = icmp ult i32 %i, %b
    %loopcond = icmp ne i1 %endcond, i32 0
    br i1 %loopcond, label %loop, label %afterloop

  afterloop:                                         ; preds = %loop
    ret i32 %addtmp
  }
```

Summary

In this chapter, you learned how to create simple LLVM IR using rich libraries
provided by LLVM. Remember that LLVM IR is an intermediate representation.
The high-level programming languages are converted to LLVM IR using the custom
parser, which breaks down the code into atomic pieces such as variables, functions,
function return type, function arguments, if-else conditions, loops, pointers, array,
and so on. These atomic elements can be stored into custom data structures and then
those data structures can be used to emit LLVM IR, as demonstrated in this chapter.

In the parser phase, syntactic analysis can be done, while lexical analysis and type
checking can be done in an intermediate stage after parsing and before emitting IR.

In practical usage, one would hardly find the IR being emitted in a hard-coded way
as demonstrated in this chapter. Instead, a language is parsed and represented in
an Abstract Syntax Tree. The tree is then used to emit LLVM IR with the help of the
LLVM library, as shown earlier. The LLVM community has provided an excellent
tutorial for writing a parser and emitting LLVM IR. You can visit `http://llvm.org/
docs/tutorial/` for the same.

In the next chapter, we will see how to emit some complex data structures such as
array, pointers. Also, we will go through some examples from Clang, the frontend
for C/C++, and understand how semantic Analysis is done.

3

Advanced LLVM IR

LLVM provides a powerful intermediate representation for efficient compiler transformations and analysis, while providing a natural means to debug and visualize the transformations. The IR is so designed that it can be easily mapped to high level languages. LLVM IR provides typed information, which can be used for various optimizations.

In the last chapter, you learned how to create some simple LLVM instructions within a function and module. Starting from simple examples such as emitting binary operations, we constructed functions in a module and also created some complex programming paradigms such as if-else and loops. LLVM provides a rich set of instructions and intrinsics to emit a complex IR.

In this chapter, we will go through some more examples of LLVM IR which involve memory operations. Some advanced topics such as aggregate data types and operations on them will also be covered. The topics covered in this chapter are as follows:

- Getting the address of an element
- Reading from the memory
- Writing into a memory location
- Inserting a scalar into a vector
- Extracting a scalar from a vector

Memory access operations

Memory is an important component of almost all computing systems. Memory stores data, which needs to be read to perform operations on the computing system. Results of the operations are stored back in the memory.

The first step is to get the location of the desired element from the memory and store the address in which that particular element can be found. You will now learn how to calculate the address and perform load-store operations.

Getting the address of an element

In LLVM, the `getelementptr` instruction is used to get the address of an element in an aggregate data structure. It only calculates the address and does not access the memory.

The first argument of the `getelementptr` instruction is a type used as the basis for calculating the address. The second argument is pointer or vector of pointers which act as base of the address - which in our array case will be a. The next arguments are the indices of the element to be accessed.

The Language reference (`http://llvm.org/docs/LangRef.html#getelementptr-instruction`) mentions important notes on `getelementptr` instruction as follows:

> *The first index always indexes the pointer value given as the first argument, the second index indexes a value of the type pointed to (not necessarily the value directly pointed to, since the first index can be non-zero), etc. The first type indexed into must be a pointer value, subsequent types can be arrays, vectors, and structs. Note that subsequent types being indexed into can never be pointers, since that would require loading the pointer before continuing calculation.*

This essentially implies two important things:

1. Every pointer has an index, and the first index is always an array index. If it's a pointer to a structure, you have to use index 0 to mean (the first such structure), then the index of the element.

2. The first type parameter helps GEP identify the sizes of the base structure and its elements, thus easily calculating the address. The resulting type (`%a1`) is not necessarily the same.

More elaborated explanation is provided at `http://llvm.org/docs/GetElementPtr.html`

Let's assume that we have a pointer to a vector of two 32 bit integers `<2 x i32>*` `%a` and we want to access second integer from the vector. The address will be calculated as

```
%a1 = getelementptr i32, <2 x i32>* %a, i32 1
```

To emit this instruction, LLVM API can be used as follows:

First create an array type which will be passed as argument to the function.

```
Function *createFunc(IRBuilder<> &Builder, std::string Name) {
  Type *u32Ty = Type::getInt32Ty(Context);
  Type *vecTy = VectorType::get(u32Ty, 2);
  Type *ptrTy = vecTy->getPointerTo(0);
  FunctionType *funcType =
      FunctionType::get(Builder.getInt32Ty(), ptrTy, false);
  Function *fooFunc =
      Function::Create(funcType, Function::ExternalLinkage, Name,
  ModuleOb);
  return fooFunc;
}


Value *getGEP(IRBuilder<> &Builder, Value *Base, Value *Offset) {
  return Builder.CreateGEP(Builder.getInt32Ty(), Base, Offset, "a1");
}
```

The whole code looks like:

```
#include "llvm/IR/IRBuilder.h"
#include "llvm/IR/LLVMContext.h"
#include "llvm/IR/Module.h"
#include "llvm/IR/Verifier.h"
#include <vector>
using namespace llvm;

static LLVMContext &Context = getGlobalContext();
static Module *ModuleOb = new Module("my compiler", Context);
static std::vector<std::string> FunArgs;

Function *createFunc(IRBuilder<> &Builder, std::string Name) {
  Type *u32Ty = Type::getInt32Ty(Context);
  Type *vecTy = VectorType::get(u32Ty, 2);
  Type *ptrTy = vecTy->getPointerTo(0);
  FunctionType *funcType =
      FunctionType::get(Builder.getInt32Ty(), ptrTy, false);
  Function *fooFunc =
      Function::Create(funcType, Function::ExternalLinkage, Name,
  ModuleOb);
  return fooFunc;
}
```

```
    void setFuncArgs(Function *fooFunc, std::vector<std::string> FunArgs)
    {
      unsigned Idx = 0;
      Function::arg_iterator AI, AE;
      for (AI = fooFunc->arg_begin(), AE = fooFunc->arg_end(); AI != AE;
           ++AI, ++Idx)
        AI->setName(FunArgs[Idx]);
    }


    BasicBlock *createBB(Function *fooFunc, std::string Name) {
      return BasicBlock::Create(Context, Name, fooFunc);
    }


    Value *getGEP(IRBuilder<> &Builder, Value *Base, Value *Offset) {
      return Builder.CreateGEP(Builder.getInt32Ty(), Base, Offset, "a1");
    }


    int main(int argc, char *argv[]) {
      FunArgs.push_back("a");
      static IRBuilder<> Builder(Context);
      Function *fooFunc = createFunc(Builder, "foo");
      setFuncArgs(fooFunc, FunArgs);
      Value *Base = fooFunc->arg_begin();
      BasicBlock *entry = createBB(fooFunc, "entry");
      Builder.SetInsertPoint(entry);
      Value *gep = getGEP(Builder, Base, Builder.getInt32(1));
      verifyFunction(*fooFunc);
      ModuleOb->dump();
      return 0;
    }
```

Compile the code

```
$ clang++ toy.cpp `llvm-config --cxxflags --ldflags --system-libs --libs
core` -fno-rtti -o toy
$ ./toy
```

Output

```
    ; ModuleID = 'my compiler'

    define i32 @foo(<2 x i32>* %a) {
    entry:
      %a1 = getelementptr i32, <2 x i32>* %a, i32 1
      ret i32 0
    }
```

Reading from the memory

Now, since we have the address, we are ready to read the data from that address and assign the read value to a variable.

In LLVM the `load` instruction is used to read from a memory location. This simple instruction or combination of similar instructions may then be mapped to some of the sophisticated memory read instructions in low-level assembly.

A `load` instruction takes an argument, which is the memory address from which the data should be read. We obtained the address in the previous section by the `getelementptr` instruction in `a1`.

The `load` instruction looks like the following:

```
%val = load i32, i32* a1
```

This means that the `load` will take the data pointed by `a1` and save in `%val`.

To emit this we can use the API provided by LLVM in a function, as shown in the following code:

```
Value *getLoad(IRBuilder<> &Builder, Value *Address) {
  return Builder.CreateLoad(Address, "load");
}
```

Let's also return the loaded value:

```
builder.CreateRet(val);
```

The whole code is as follows:

```
#include "llvm/IR/IRBuilder.h"
#include "llvm/IR/LLVMContext.h"
#include "llvm/IR/Module.h"
#include "llvm/IR/Verifier.h"
#include <vector>
using namespace llvm;

static LLVMContext &Context = getGlobalContext();
static Module *ModuleOb = new Module("my compiler", Context);
static std::vector<std::string> FunArgs;

Function *createFunc(IRBuilder<> &Builder, std::string Name) {
  Type *u32Ty = Type::getInt32Ty(Context);
  Type *vecTy = VectorType::get(u32Ty, 2);
  Type *ptrTy = vecTy->getPointerTo(0);
```

```
    FunctionType *funcType =
        FunctionType::get(Builder.getInt32Ty(), ptrTy, false);
    Function *fooFunc =
        Function::Create(funcType, Function::ExternalLinkage, Name,
    ModuleOb);
    return fooFunc;
}


void setFuncArgs(Function *fooFunc, std::vector<std::string>
FunArgs) {
    unsigned Idx = 0;
    Function::arg_iterator AI, AE;
    for (AI = fooFunc->arg_begin(), AE = fooFunc->arg_end(); AI != AE;
        ++AI, ++Idx)
        AI->setName(FunArgs[Idx]);
}


BasicBlock *createBB(Function *fooFunc, std::string Name) {
    return BasicBlock::Create(Context, Name, fooFunc);
}


Value *getGEP(IRBuilder<> &Builder, Value *Base, Value *Offset) {
    return Builder.CreateGEP(Builder.getInt32Ty(), Base, Offset, "a1");
}


Value *getLoad(IRBuilder<> &Builder, Value *Address) {
    return Builder.CreateLoad(Address, "load");
}


int main(int argc, char *argv[]) {
    FunArgs.push_back("a");
    static IRBuilder<> Builder(Context);
    Function *fooFunc = createFunc(Builder, "foo");
    setFuncArgs(fooFunc, FunArgs);
    Value *Base = fooFunc->arg_begin();
    BasicBlock *entry = createBB(fooFunc, "entry");
    Builder.SetInsertPoint(entry);
    Value *gep = getGEP(Builder, Base, Builder.getInt32(1));
    Value *load = getLoad(Builder, gep);
    Builder.CreateRet(load);
    verifyFunction(*fooFunc);
    ModuleOb->dump();
    return 0;
}
```

Compile the following code:

```
$ clang++ toy.cpp `llvm-config --cxxflags --ldflags --system-libs
--libs core` -fno-rtti -o toy
$ ./toy
```

The following is the output:

```
; ModuleID = 'my compiler'

define i32 @foo(<2 x i32>* %a) {
entry:
  %a1 = getelementptr i32, <2 x i32>* %a, i32 1
  %load = load i32, i32* %a1
  ret i32 %load
}
```

Writing into a memory location

LLVM uses the store instruction to write into a memory location. There are two arguments to the store instruction: a value to store and an address at which to store it. The store instruction has no return value. Let's say that we want to write a data to the second element of the vector of two integers. The store instruction looks like store i32 3, i32* %a1. To emit the store instruction, we can use the following API provided by LLVM:

```
void getStore(IRBuilder<> &Builder, Value *Address, Value *V) {
  Builder.CreateStore(V, Address);
}
```

For example, we will multiply the second element of the <2 x i32> vector by 16 and store it back at the same location.

Consider the following code:

```
#include "llvm/IR/IRBuilder.h"
#include "llvm/IR/LLVMContext.h"
#include "llvm/IR/Module.h"
#include "llvm/IR/Verifier.h"
#include <vector>
using namespace llvm;

static LLVMContext &Context = getGlobalContext();
static Module *ModuleOb = new Module("my compiler", Context);
static std::vector<std::string> FunArgs;
```

```
Function *createFunc(IRBuilder<> &Builder, std::string Name) {
  Type *u32Ty = Type::getInt32Ty(Context);
  Type *vecTy = VectorType::get(u32Ty, 2);
  Type *ptrTy = vecTy->getPointerTo(0);
  FunctionType *funcType =
      FunctionType::get(Builder.getInt32Ty(), ptrTy, false);
  Function *fooFunc =
      Function::Create(funcType, Function::ExternalLinkage, Name,
  ModuleOb);
  return fooFunc;
}

void setFuncArgs(Function *fooFunc, std::vector<std::string> FunArgs)
{
  unsigned Idx = 0;
  Function::arg_iterator AI, AE;
  for (AI = fooFunc->arg_begin(), AE = fooFunc->arg_end(); AI != AE;
       ++AI, ++Idx)
    AI->setName(FunArgs[Idx]);
}

BasicBlock *createBB(Function *fooFunc, std::string Name) {
  return BasicBlock::Create(Context, Name, fooFunc);
}

Value *createArith(IRBuilder<> &Builder, Value *L, Value *R) {
  return Builder.CreateMul(L, R, "multmp");
}

Value *getGEP(IRBuilder<> &Builder, Value *Base, Value *Offset) {
  return Builder.CreateGEP(Builder.getInt32Ty(), Base, Offset, "a1");
}

Value *getLoad(IRBuilder<> &Builder, Value *Address) {
  return Builder.CreateLoad(Address, "load");
}

void getStore(IRBuilder<> &Builder, Value *Address, Value *V) {
  Builder.CreateStore(V, Address);
}

int main(int argc, char *argv[]) {
  FunArgs.push_back("a");
  static IRBuilder<> Builder(Context);
```

```
    Function *fooFunc = createFunc(Builder, "foo");
    setFuncArgs(fooFunc, FunArgs);
    Value *Base = fooFunc->arg_begin();
    BasicBlock *entry = createBB(fooFunc, "entry");
    Builder.SetInsertPoint(entry);
    Value *gep = getGEP(Builder, Base, Builder.getInt32(1));
    Value *load = getLoad(Builder, gep);
    Value *constant = Builder.getInt32(16);
    Value *val = createArith(Builder, load, constant);
    getStore(Builder, gep, val);
    Builder.CreateRet(val);
    verifyFunction(*fooFunc);
    ModuleOb->dump();
    return 0;
}
```

Compile the following code:

```
$ clang++ toy.cpp `llvm-config --cxxflags --ldflags --system-libs
--libs core` -fno-rtti -o toy
$ ./toy
```

The resulting output will be as follows:

```
; ModuleID = 'my compiler'

define i32 @foo(<2 x i32>* %a) {
entry:
  %a1 = getelementptr i32, <2 x i32>* %a, i32 1
  %load = load i32, i32* %a1
  %multmp = mul i32 %load, 16
  store i32 %multmp, i32* %a1
  ret i32 %multmp
}
```

Inserting a scalar into a vector

LLVM also provides the API to emit an instruction, which inserts a scalar into a vector type. Note that this vector is different from an array. A vector type is a simple derived type that represents a vector of elements. Vector types are used when multiple primitive data are operated in parallel using **single instruction multiple data (SIMD)**. A vector type requires a size (number of elements) and an underlying primitive data type. For example, we have a vector Vec that has four integers of i32 type <4 x i32>. Now, we want to insert the values 10, 20, 30, and 40 at 0, 1, 2, and 3 indexes of the vector.

The `insertelement` instruction takes three arguments. The first argument is a value of vector type. The second operand is a scalar value whose type must equal the element type of the first operand. The third operand is an index indicating the position at which to insert the value. The resultant value is a vector of the same type.

The `insertelement` instruction looks like the following:

```
%vec0 = insertelement <4 x double> Vec, %val0, %idx
```

This can be further understood by keeping the following in mind:

- `Vec` is of vector type `< 4 x i32 >`
- `val0` is the value to be inserted
- `idx` is the index at which the value is to be inserted in the vector

Consider the following code:

```cpp
#include "llvm/IR/IRBuilder.h"
#include "llvm/IR/LLVMContext.h"
#include "llvm/IR/Module.h"
#include "llvm/IR/Verifier.h"
#include <vector>
using namespace llvm;

static LLVMContext &Context = getGlobalContext();
static Module *ModuleOb = new Module("my compiler", Context);
static std::vector<std::string> FunArgs;

Function *createFunc(IRBuilder<> &Builder, std::string Name) {
  Type *u32Ty = Type::getInt32Ty(Context);
  Type *vecTy = VectorType::get(u32Ty, 4);
  FunctionType *funcType =
      FunctionType::get(Builder.getInt32Ty(), vecTy, false);
  Function *fooFunc =
      Function::Create(funcType, Function::ExternalLinkage, Name,
  ModuleOb);
  return fooFunc;
}

void setFuncArgs(Function *fooFunc, std::vector<std::::string>
FunArgs) {
  unsigned Idx = 0;
  Function::arg_iterator AI, AE;
```

```
    for (AI = fooFunc->arg_begin(), AE = fooFunc->arg_end(); AI != AE;
         ++AI, ++Idx)
      AI->setName(FunArgs[Idx]);
  }


BasicBlock *createBB(Function *fooFunc, std::string Name) {
    return BasicBlock::Create(Context, Name, fooFunc);
  }


Value *getInsertElement(IRBuilder<> &Builder, Value *Vec, Value *Val,
                        Value *Index) {
    return Builder.CreateInsertElement(Vec, Val, Index);
  }


int main(int argc, char *argv[]) {
    FunArgs.push_back("a");
    static IRBuilder<> Builder(Context);
    Function *fooFunc = createFunc(Builder, "foo");
    setFuncArgs(fooFunc, FunArgs);

    BasicBlock *entry = createBB(fooFunc, "entry");
    Builder.SetInsertPoint(entry);

    Value *Vec = fooFunc->arg_begin();
    for (unsigned int i = 0; i < 4; i++)
      Value *V = getInsertElement(Builder, Vec,
      Builder.getInt32((i + 1) * 10), Builder.getInt32(i));

    Builder.CreateRet(Builder.getInt32(0));
    verifyFunction(*fooFunc);
    ModuleOb->dump();
    return 0;
  }
```

Compile the following code:

```
$ clang++ toy.cpp `llvm-config --cxxflags --ldflags --system-libs
--libs core` -fno-rtti -o toy
$ ./toy
```

The resulting output is as follows:

```
; ModuleID = 'my compiler'

define i32 @foo(<4 x i32> %a) {
entry:
  %0 = insertelement <4 x i32> %a, i32 10, i32 0
  %1 = insertelement <4 x i32> %a, i32 20, i32 1
  %2 = insertelement <4 x i32> %a, i32 30, i32 2
  %3 = insertelement <4 x i32> %a, i32 40, i32 3
  ret i32 0
}
```

The vector `Vec` will have `<10, 20, 30, 40>` values.

Extracting a scalar from a vector

An individual scalar element can be extracted from a vector. LLVM provides the `extractelement` instruction for the same. The first operand of an `extractelement` instruction is a value of vector type. The second operand is an index indicating the position from which to extract the element.

The `extractelement` instruction looks like the following:

```
result = extractelement <4 x i32> %vec, i32 %idx
```

This can be further understood by keeping the following in mind:

- `vec` is a vector
- `idx` is the index at which the data to be extracted lies
- `result` is of scalar type, which is `i32` here

Let's take an example where we want to add all the elements of a given vector and return an integer.

Consider the follwing code:

```
#include "llvm/IR/IRBuilder.h"
#include "llvm/IR/LLVMContext.h"
#include "llvm/IR/Module.h"
#include "llvm/IR/Verifier.h"
#include <vector>
using namespace llvm;
```

```cpp
static LLVMContext &Context = getGlobalContext();
static Module *ModuleOb = new Module("my compiler", Context);
static std::vector<std::string> FunArgs;

Function *createFunc(IRBuilder<> &Builder, std::string Name) {
  Type *u32Ty = Type::getInt32Ty(Context);
  Type *vecTy = VectorType::get(u32Ty, 4);
  FunctionType *funcType =
      FunctionType::get(Builder.getInt32Ty(), vecTy, false);
  Function *fooFunc =
      Function::Create(funcType, Function::ExternalLinkage, Name,
  ModuleOb);
  return fooFunc;
}

void setFuncArgs(Function *fooFunc, std::vector<std::string>
FunArgs) {
  unsigned Idx = 0;
  Function::arg_iterator AI, AE;
  for (AI = fooFunc->arg_begin(), AE = fooFunc->arg_end(); AI != AE;
       ++AI, ++Idx)
    AI->setName(FunArgs[Idx]);
}

BasicBlock *createBB(Function *fooFunc, std::string Name) {
  return BasicBlock::Create(Context, Name, fooFunc);
}

Value *createArith(IRBuilder<> &Builder, Value *L, Value *R) {
  return Builder.CreateAdd(L, R, "add");
}

Value *getExtractElement(IRBuilder<> &Builder, Value *Vec, Value
*Index) {
  return Builder.CreateExtractElement(Vec, Index);
}

int main(int argc, char *argv[]) {
  FunArgs.push_back("a");
  static IRBuilder<> Builder(Context);
  Function *fooFunc = createFunc(Builder, "foo");
  setFuncArgs(fooFunc, FunArgs);
```

```
    BasicBlock *entry = createBB(fooFunc, "entry");
    Builder.SetInsertPoint(entry);

    Value *Vec = fooFunc->arg_begin();
    SmallVector<Value *, 4> V;
    for (unsigned int i = 0; i < 4; i++)
      V[i] = getExtractElement(Builder, Vec, Builder.getInt32(i));

    Value *add1 = createArith(Builder, V[0], V[1]);
    Value *add2 = createArith(Builder, add1, V[2]);
    Value *add = createArith(Builder, add2, V[3]);

    Builder.CreateRet(add);
    verifyFunction(*fooFunc);
    ModuleOb->dump();
    return 0;
}
```

Compile the following code:

```
$ clang++ toy.cpp `llvm-config --cxxflags --ldflags --system-libs
--libs core` -fno-rtti -o toy
$ ./toy
```

Output:

```
ModuleID = 'my compiler'

define i32 @foo(<4 x i32> %a) {
entry:
  %0 = extractelement <4 x i32> %a, i32 0
  %1 = extractelement <4 x i32> %a, i32 1
  %2 = extractelement <4 x i32> %a, i32 2
  %3 = extractelement <4 x i32> %a, i32 3
  %add = add i32 %0, %1
  %add1 = add i32 %add, %2
  %add2 = add i32 %add1, %3
  ret i32 %add2
}
```

Summary

Memory operations form an important instruction for most of the target architecture. Some of the architectures have sophisticated instructions to move data in and out of the memory. Some even perform binary operations directly on the memory operands, while some of them load data from memory into registers and then perform operations on them (CISC vs RISC). Many load-store operations are also done by LLVM instrinsics. For examples, please refer to `http://llvm.org/docs/` `LangRef.html#masked-vector-load-and-store-intrinsics`.

LLVM IR provides a common playfield for all the architectures. It provides elementary instructions for data operations on memory or on aggregate data types. The architectures, while lowering LLVM IR, may combine IR instructions to emit their specific instructions. In this chapter, we went through some advanced IR instructions and also looked into examples of them. For a detailed study, refer to `http://llvm.org/docs/LangRef.html`, which provides the authoritative resource for LLVM IR instructions.

In the next chapter, you will study how LLVM IR can be optimized to reduce instructions and emit a clean code.

4
Basic IR Transformations

Until now, we have seen how the IR is independent of its target and how it can be used to generate code for a specific backend. To generate efficient code for the backend, we optimize the IR generated by the frontend by running a series of analysis and transformation passes using the LLVM pass manager. We must note that most of the optimizations that happen in a compiler take place on the IR, one of the reasons being that the IR is retargetable and the same set of optimizations would be valid for a number of targets. It reduces the effort of writing the same optimization for every target. There are some target-specific optimizations too; they happen at the selection DAG level, which we will see later. Another reason for IR being the target of optimization is that LLVM IR is in SSA form, which means every variable is assigned only once and every new assignment to a variable is a new variable itself. One very visible benefit of this representation is that we don't have to do reaching definition analysis where some variable is assigned a value of another variable. SSA representation also helps in a number of optimizations such as constant propagation, dead code elimination, and so on. Going ahead, we will see some of the important optimizations in LLVM, what is the role of LLVM Pass Infrastructure, and how we can use the opt tool to perform different optimizations.

In this chapter, we will cover following topics:

- The opt tool
- Pass and Pass Manager
- Using other Pass info in own pass
- IR simplification examples
- IR combination examples

Opt Tool

Opt is the LLVM Optimizer and analyzer tool that is run on LLVM IR to optimize the IR or produce an analysis about it. We saw in the first chapter a very basic introduction to the opt tool, and how to use it to run analysis and transformation passes. In this section, we will see what else the opt tool does. We must note that opt is a developer tool and all the optimizations that it provides can be invoked from the frontend as well.

With the opt tool, we can specify the level of optimization that we need, which means we can specify the optimization levels from 00, 01, 02, to 03(00 being the least optimized code and 03 being the most optimized code). Apart from these, there is also an optimization level Os or Oz, which deals with space optimization. The syntax to invoke one of these optimizations is:

```
$ opt -Ox -S input.ll
```

Here, x represents the optimization level, which can have a value from 0 to 3 or s or z. These optimization levels are similar to what Clang frontend specifies. -00 represents no optimization whereas –01 means only few optimizations are enabled. –02 is a moderate level of optimization and –03 is the highest level of optimization, which is similar to –02 but it allows optimization that takes longer to perform or may generate larger code (the O3 level does not guarantee that the code will be the most optimized and efficient, it just says that the compiler will try more to optimize the code and in the process may break things also). –0s means optimization for size, basically not running optimizations which increase code size (for example, it removes `slp-vectorizer` optimization) and perform optimizations that reduce code size (for example, instruction combining optimization).

We can direct the opt tool to run a specific pass that we require. These passes can be one of the already defined passes listed at `http://llvm.org/docs/Passes.html` or one of the passes we have written ourselves. The passes listed in the above link are also run in the optimization levels of -01, -02, and -03. To view which pass is being run at a certain optimization level, use the `-debug-pass=Structure` command-line option along with the opt tool.

Let's take an example to demonstrate the difference between the O1 and O2 level of optimization. The O3 level generally has one or two more passes from O2. So, let's take an example and see how much the O2 level of optimization optimizes the code. Write the test code in the `test.ll` file:

```
define internal i32 @test(i32* %X, i32* %Y)
{
    %A = load i32, i32* %X
    %B = load i32, i32* %Y
    %C = add i32 %A, %B
    ret i32 %C
}
define internal i32 @caller(i32* %B)
{
    %A = alloca i32
    store i32 1, i32* %A
    %C = call i32 @test(i32* %A, i32* %B)
    ret i32 %C
}
define i32 @callercaller()
{
    %B = alloca i32
    store i32 2, i32* %B
    %X = call i32 @caller(i32* %B)
    ret i32 %X
}
```

In this test code, the `callercaller` function calls the `caller` function, which in turn calls the `test` function, which performs an addition of two numbers and returns the value to its caller, which in turn returns the value to the `callercaller` function.

Now, run the O1 and O2 levels of optimization, as shown:

```
$ opt -O1 -S test.ll > 1.ll
$ opt -O2 -S test.ll > 2.ll
```

The following screenshot shows the difference in the optimized code for the O1 and O2 levels:

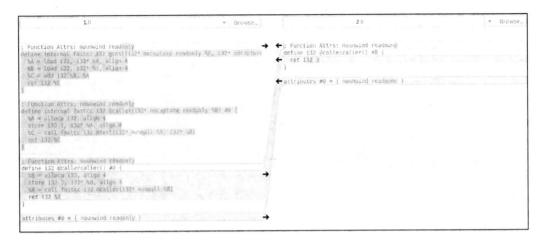

As we can see, the code in O2 has optimized the calls to the function and the Add operations as well and returns the result directly from the `callercaller` function. This is obtained due to the fact that O2 optimization runs the passes **always-inline** which inlines all the function calls and treats the code as one big function. Then, in also runs the `globaldce` pass, which eliminates unreachable internals from the code. After this, it runs `constmerge` which merges duplicate global constants into a single constant. It also performs a global value numbering pass that eliminates partially or fully redundant instructions and eliminates redundant load instructions.

Pass and Pass Manager

LLVM's `Pass` infrastructure is one of the many important features of the LLVM system. There are a number of analysis and optimization passes that can be run using this infrastructure. The starting point for LLVM passes is the `Pass` class, which is a superclass of all the passes. We need to inherit from some predefined subclasses taking into account what our pass is going to implement.

- **ModulePass**: This is the most general superclass. By inheriting this class we allow the entire module to be analyzed at once. The functions within the module may not be referred to in a particular order. To use it, write a subclass that inherits from the `ModulePass` subclass and overloads the `runOnModule` function.

Before going ahead with the discussion of other `Pass` classes, let's look into the three virtual methods that the `Pass` classes override:

- **doInitialization**: This is meant to do initialization stuff that does not depend on the current function being processed.
- **runOn{Passtype}**: This is the method where we should implement our subclass for the functionality of the pass. This will be `runOnFunction` for `FunctionPass`, `runOnLoop` for `LoopPass`, and so on.
- **doFinalization**: This is called when `runOn{Passtype}` has finished doing the job for every function in the program.

- **FunctionPass**: These passes execute on each function present in the module, independent from other functions in the module. There is no defined order in which the functions will be processed. They are not allowed to modify functions other than the one being processed, and any addition or deletion of functions from the current module is also not allowed. To implement `FunctionPass` we might need to overload the three virtual functions mentioned earlier by implementing in the `runOnFunction` method.

- **BasicBlockPass**: These passes work on basic blocks one at a time, independently of other basic blocks present in the program. They are not allowed to add or delete any new basic block or change the CFG. They are also not allowed to do things that `FunctionPass` is not allowed to. To implement, they can override the `doInitialization` and `doFinalization` methods of `FunctionPass`, or overload their own virtual methods for the two methods mentioned earlier and the `runOnBasicBlock` method.

- **LoopPass**: These passes work on each loop in the function, independent of all other loops within the function. Loops are processed in such a way that the outermost loop is executed the last. To implement `LoopPass` we need to overload the `doInitialization`, `doFinalization`, and `runOnLoop` methods.

Now, let's see how to get started with writing a custom pass. Let's write a pass that will print the names of all the functions.

Before getting started with writing the implementation of the pass, we need to make changes in a few places in the code so that the pass is recognized and can be run.

We need to create a directory under the LLVM tree. Let's make a directory, `lib/Transforms/FnNamePrint`. In this directory, we need to create a `Makefile` with the following contents, which will allow our pass to be compiled:

```
LEVEL = ../../..

LIBRARYNAME = FnNamePrint

LOADABLE_MODULE = 1

include $(LEVEL)/Makefile.common
```

This specifies that all `.cpp` files should be compiled and linked into a shared object that will be available in the `lib` folder of the `build-folder` (`build-folder/lib/FnNamePrint.so`).

Now, let's get started with writing the actual pass implementation. We need to create the source file for the pass in `lib/Transforms/FnNamePrint`: let's name it `FnNamePrint.cpp`. The first step now is to choose the correct subclass. In this case, as we are trying to print names of each function, the `FunctionPass` class will serve our purpose by processing one function at a time. Also, we are only printing the name of function and not modifying anything within it, so we are choosing `FunctionPass` for simplicity. We could use `ModulePass` as well because it is an `Immutable Pass`.

Now, let's write the source code for the pass implementation, which looks like this:

```
#include "llvm/Pass.h"
#include "llvm/IR/Function.h"
#include "llvm/Support/raw_ostream.h"

using namespace llvm;

namespace {
  struct FnNamePrint: public FunctionPass {
    static char ID;
    FnNamePrint () : FunctionPass(ID) {}
    bool runOnFunction(Function &F) override {
      errs() << "Function " << F.getName() << '\n';
      return false;
    }
  };
}
```

```
char FnNamePrint::ID = 0;
static RegisterPass< FnNamePrint > X("funcnameprint",
"Function Name Print", false, false);
```

In the preceding code we include the necessary headers first and use an llvm namespace:

```
#include "llvm/Pass.h"
#include "llvm/IR/Function.h"
#include "llvm/Support/raw_ostream.h"

using namespace llvm;
```

We declare our pass as a structure, FnNamePrint, which is a subclass of FunctionPass. In runOnFunction we implement the logic to print the function name. The bool value returned in the end signifies whether we have made any modification within the function. A True value is returned if some modifications was made, otherwise, false is returned. In our case, we are not making any modifications, so we return false.

```
struct FnNamePrint: public FunctionPass {
  static char ID;
  FnNamePrint () : FunctionPass(ID) {}
  bool runOnFunction(Function &F) override {
    errs() << "Function " << F.getName() << '\n';
    return false;
    }
  };
}
```

Then, we declare the ID for the pass, which is used to identify the pass:

```
char FnNamePrint::ID = 0;
```

Finally, we need to register the passes with the Pass Manager. The first argument is the Pass name used by the opt tool to identify this pass. The second argument is the actual Pass name. The third and fourth arguments specify whether the pass modified the cfg and whether it is an analysis pass.

```
static RegisterPass< FnNamePrint > X("funcnameprint",
"Function Name Print", false, false);
```

 The implementation of the pass is done. Now, before we use it, we need to build LLVM using the make command, which will build the shared object in the lib folder within the build (build-folder/lib/FnNamePrint.so).

Now, we can run the pass over a test case using the `opt` tool in the following way:

```
$ opt -load path-to-llvm/build/lib/FnNamePrint.so -funcnameprint
test.ll
```

The `load` command line option specifies the path from where to pick the shared object of the pass and `-funcnameprint` is the option to opt tool to tell it to run the pass we have written. The Pass will print the names of all the function present in the testcase. For the example in the first section it will print out:

```
Function test
Function caller
Function callercaller
```

So, we got started with writing a Pass. Now, we will see the significance of the `PassManager` class in LLVM.

The `PassManager` class schedules the passes to be run efficiently. The `PassManager` is used by all LLVM tools that run passes for the execution of these passes. It is the responsibility of the `PassManager` to make sure the interaction between the passes is correctly done. As it tries to execute the passes in an optimized way, it must have information regarding how the passes interact with each other and what the different dependencies between the passes are.

A pass itself can specify the dependency on other passes, that is, which passes need to be run before the execution of the current pass. Also, it can specify the passes that will be invalidated by the execution of the current pass. The `PassManager` gets the analysis results before a pass is executed. We will later see how a pass can specify such dependencies.

The main work of the `PassManager` is to avoid the calculation of analysis results time and again. This is done by keeping track of which analyses are available, which are invalidated, and which analyses are required. The `PassManager` tracks the lifetimes of the analysis results and frees the memory holding the analysis results when not required, allowing for optimal memory use.

The `PassManager` pipelines the passes together to get better memory and cache results, improving the cache behavior of the compiler. When a series of consecutive `FunctionPass` are given, it will execute all the `FunctionPass` on the first function, then all the `FunctionPass` on the second function, and so on. This improves cache behavior as it is only dealing with the single function part of the LLVM representation and not the entire program.

The `PassManager` also specifies the `-debug-pass` option with which we can see how one pass interacts with other passes. We can see what all passes are run using the `-debug-pass=Argument` option. We can use the `-debug-pass=Structure` option to see how the passes had run. It will also give us the names of the passes that ran. Let's take the example of the test code in the first section of this chapter:

```
$ opt -O2 -S test.ll -debug-pass=Structure
$ opt -load /build-folder/lib/LLVMFnNamePrint.so test.ll -funcnameprint
-debug-pass=Structure


Pass Arguments:  -targetlibinfo -tti -funcnameprint -verify
Target Library Information
Target Transform Information
  ModulePass Manager
    FunctionPass Manager
      Function Name Print
      Module Verifier
Function test
Function caller
Function callercaller
```

In the output, the `Pass Arguments` gives us the passes that are run and the following list is the structure used to run each pass. The Passes just after `ModulePass Manager` will show the passes run per module (here, it is empty). The passes in hierarchy of `FunctionPass Manager` show that these passes were run per function (`Function Name Print` and `Module Verifier`), which is the expected result.

The `PassManger` also provides some other useful flags, some of which are the following:

- **time-passes**: This gives time information about the pass along with the other passes that are lined up.

- **stats**: This prints statistics about each pass.

- **instcount**: This collects the count of all instructions and reports them. `-stats` must also be Passes to the opt tool so that the results of `instcount` are visible.

Using other Pass info in current Pass

For the Pass Manager to work optimally it needs to know the dependencies between the Passes. Each of the passes can itself declare its dependencies: the analysis passes that need to be executed before this pass is executed and the passes that will get invalidated after the current pass is run. To specify these dependencies, a pass needs to implement the `getAnalysisUsage` method.

```
virtual void getAnalysisUsage(AnalysisUsage &Info) const;
```

Using this method the current pass can specify the required and invalidated sets by filling in the details in the AnalysisUsage object. To fill in the information the Pass needs to call any of the following methods:

AnalysisUsage::addRequired<> method

This method arranges for the execution of a Pass prior to the current Pass. One example of this is: for memory copy optimization it needs the results of an alias analysis:

```
void getAnalysisUsage(AnalysisUsage &AU) const override {
AU.addRequired<AliasAnalysis>();
...
...
}
```

By adding the pass required to run, it is made sure that Alias Analysis Pass is run before the MemCpyOpt Pass. Also, this makes sure that if the Alias Analysis has been invalidated by some other Pass, it will be run before the MemCpyOpt Pass is run.

AnalysisUsage:addRequiredTransitive<> method

When an analysis chains to other analyses for results, this method should be used instead of the addRequired method. That is, when we need to preserve the order in which the analysis passes are run we use this method. For example:

```
void DependenceAnalysis::getAnalysisUsage(AnalysisUsage &AU) const
{
  ...
  AU.addRequiredTransitive<AliasAnalysis>();
  AU.addRequiredTransitive<ScalarEvolution>();
  AU.addRequiredTransitive<LoopInfo>();
}
```

Here, DependenceAnalysis chains to AliasAnalysis, ScalarEvolution and LoopInfo Passes for the results.

AnalysisUsage::addPreserved<> method

By using this method a Pass can specify which analyses of other Passes it will not invalidate on running: that is, it will preserve the information already present, if any. This means that the subsequent passes that require the analysis would not need to run this again.

For example, in the case of the `MemCpyOpt` Pass seen earlier, it required the `AliasAnalysis` results and it also preserved them. Also:

```
void getAnalysisUsage(AnalysisUsage &AU) const override {
    ......
    AU.addPreserved<AliasAnalysis>();
    .....
}
```

To get a detailed understanding of how everything is linked and works together, you can pick up any of the transformation passes and go through the source code and you will know how they are getting information from other passes and how they are using it.

Instruction simplification example

In this section, we will see how we fold instructions into simpler forms in LLVM. Here, the creation of new instructions will not take place. Instruction simplification does constant folding:

```
sub i32 2, 1 -> 1
```

That is, it simplifies the `sub` instruction to a constant value 1.

It can handle non-constant operands as well:

```
or i32 %x, 0 -> %x
```

It returns a value of variable `%x`

```
and i32 %x %x -> %x
```

In this case, it returns an already existing value.

The implementations for the methods that simplify instructions are located in `lib/Analysis/InstructionSimplify.cpp`.

Some of the important methods of dealing with the simplification of instructions are:

- **SimplifyBinOp method**: This is used to simplify binary operations such as addition, subtraction, and multiplication, and so on. It has the function signature as follows:

```
static Value *SimplifyBinOp(unsigned Opcode, Value *LHS,
Value *RHS, const Query &Q, unsigned MaxRecurse)
```

Here, by Opcode, we mean the operator instruction that we are trying to simplify. LHS and RHS are the operands on either side of the operator. MaxRecurse is the recursion level we specify after which the routine must stop trying simplification of the instruction.

In this method, we have a switch case on the Opcode:

```
switch (Opcode) {
```

Using this Opcode, the method decides which function it needs to call for simplification. Some of the methods are as follows:

- **SimplifyAddInst**: This method tries to fold the result of the Add operator when the operands are known. Some of the folding is as follows:

```
X + undef -> undef
X + 0 -> X
X + (Y - X) -> Y or (Y - X) + X -> Y
```

The code for the last simplification in the function static Value *SimplifyAddInst(Value *Op0, Value *Op1, bool isNSW, bool isNUW, const Query &Q, unsigned MaxRecurse) looks something like this:

```
if (match(Op1, m_Sub(m_Value(Y), m_Specific(Op0))) ||
      match(Op0, m_Sub(m_Value(Y), m_Specific(Op1))))
    return Y;
```

Here, the first condition matches the (Y-X) value in the expression as Operand1: m_Value(Y) denotes value of Y and m_Specific(Op0) denotes X. As soon as it is matched it folds the expression to a constant value Y and returns it. The case is similar for the second part of our condition:

- **SimplifySubInst**: This method tries to fold the result of subtract operator when the operators are known. Some examples for the same are as follows:

```
X - undef -> undef
X - X -> 0
X - 0 -> X
X - (X - Y) -> Y
```

The matching of instructions and folding is done similar to as shown in SimplifyAddInst:

- **SimplifyAndInst**: Similar to the two preceding methods, it tries to fold the result for the logical operator And. Some examples of this are:

```
A & ~A  =  ~A & A  =  0
```

The code for this, in the method looks like:

```
if (match(Op0, m_Not(m_Specific(Op1))) ||
        match(Op1, m_Not(m_Specific(Op0))))
    return Constant::getNullValue(Op0->getType());
```

Here, it tries to match A and ~A and returns a Null value, 0, when it matches the condition.

So, we have seen a bit of instruction simplification. Now, what do we do if we can replace a set of instructions with a more effective set of instructions?

Instruction Combining

Instruction combining is a LLVM Pass and compiler technique in which we replace a sequence of instructions with instructions that are more effective and give the same result on execution in a smaller number of machine cycles. Instruction combining does not alter the CFG of the program and is mainly used for algebraic simplification. The major difference between instruction combining and instruction simplification is that in instruction simplification we cannot generate new instructions, which is possible in instruction combining. This pass is run by specifying the -instcombine argument to the opt tool and is implemented in the lib/transforms/instcombine folder. The instcombine Pass combines

```
%Y = add i32 %X, 1
%Z = add i32 %Y, 1
into:
%Z = add i32 %X, 2
```

It has removed one redundant add instruction and hence combined the two add instructions to one.

The LLVM page states that this pass guarantees that the following canonicalizations are performed on the program:

- Constant operand of a binary operator is moved to RHS.
- Bitwise operators with constant operands are grouped together with shifts being performed first then 'or' operations, 'and' operations and then 'xor operations'
- If possible, comparison operators are converted from <,>,<=,>= to == or != .
- All cmp instructions operating on Boolean values are replaced with logical operations.
- Add X, X is represented by X*2 , that is X<<1
- Multipliers with a power-of-two constant argument are transformed into shifts.

This pass starts from bool InstCombiner::runOnFunction(Function &F) located in the InstructionCombining.cpp file. There are different files under the lib/Transform/InstCombine folder to combine instructions related to different instructions. The methods, before trying to combine instructions, try to simplify them. Some of these methods for simplification of the instcombine module are:

- **SimplifyAssociativeOrCommutative function**: It performs simplification for operators that are associative or commutative. For commutative operators, it orders the operands from right to left in the order of increasing complexity. For associative operations of the form "(X op Y) op Z", it converts it to "X op (Y op Z)" if (Y op Z) can be simplified.

- **tryFactorization function**: This method tries to simplify binary operations by factoring out common terms using commutative and distributive property of the operator. For example, (A*B)+(A*C) is simplified to A*(B+C).

Now, let's look at instruction combining. As described earlier, various functionalities are implemented in different files. Let's take an example testcode and see where to add code so that instruction combining happens for our testcode.

Let's write the testcode in test.ll for the pattern (A | (B ^ C)) ^ ((A ^ C) ^ B), which can be reduced to (A & (B ^ C)):

```
define i32 @testfunc(i32 %x, i32 %y, i32 %z) {
%xor1 = xor i32 %y, %z
%or = or i32 %x, %xor1
%xor2 = xor i32 %x, %z
%xor3 = xor i32 %xor2, %y
%res = xor i32 %or, %xor3
ret i32 %res
}
```

The code in LLVM for the handling of operators such as "And", "Or", and "Xor" lies in the lib/Transforms/InstCombine/InstCombineAndOrXor.cpp file.

In the InstCombineAndOrXor.cpp file, in the InstCombiner::visitXor(BinaryOperator &I) function, go to the if condition If (Op0I && Op1I) and add the following snippet of code:

```
If (match(Op01, m_Or(m_Xor(m_Value(B), m_Value(C)), m_Value(A)))
&& match(Op1I, m_Xor( m_Xor(m_Specific(A), m_Specific(C)), m_
Specific(B)))) {
   return BinaryOperator::CreateAnd(A, Builder->CreateXor(B,C));
}
```

As it is quite clear, the code added is to match the pattern (A | (B ^ C)) ^ ((A ^ C) ^ B) and return (A & (B ^ C)) when matched.

To test the code, build LLVM and run the instcombine Pass with this test code and see the output.

```
$ opt -instcombine -S test.ll
define i32 @testfunc(i32 %x, i32 %y, i32 %z) {
%1 = xor i32 %y, %z
%res = and i32 %1, %x
ret i32 %res
}
```

So the output shows that now only one xor and one and operation is required instead of four xor and one or earlier.

To understand and add more transformations you can look into the source code in the InstCombine folder.

Summary

So, in this chapter, we looked into how simple transformations can be applied to IR. We looked into the opt tool, LLVM Pass infrastructure, the Passmanager and how to use information of one Pass in another Pass. We ended the chapter with examples of instruction simplification and instruction combining. In the next chapter, we will see some more advanced optimizations like Loop Optimization, Scalar Evolution, and others, where we will operate at a block of code rather than individual instructions.

5
Advanced IR Block Transformations

In the previous chapter, we have gone through some of the optimizations, which were mainly at instruction level. In this chapter, we will look at optimizations on block level where we will be optimizing a block of code to a simpler form, which makes the code more effective. We will start by looking at how loops are represented in LLVM, use the concept of dominance and CFG to optimize loops. We will use **Loop Simplification** (`LoopSimplify`)and **Loop Invariant Code Motion** optimizations for loop processing. We will then see how a scalar value changes during program execution and how the result of this **Scalar Evolution Optimization** can be used in other optimizations. Then we will look into how LLVM represents its in build functions called as LLVM intrinsics. Finally, we will look into how LLVM deals with concepts of parallelism by understanding its approach towards vectorization.

In this chapter, we will look into the following topics:

- Loop processing
- Scalar evolution
- LLVM intrinsics
- Vectorization

Loop processing

Before getting started with loop processing and optimization, we must have a little heads up about the concepts of CFG and dominance information. A CFG is the control flow graph of the program that gives a look into how the program may be executed through the various basic blocks. By dominance information, we get to know about the relation between the various basic blocks in the CFG.

In a CFG, we say a node d dominates a node n if every path (from the input towards output) that passes through n must also pass through d. This is denoted by d -> n. The graph G = (V, E), where V is the set of basic blocks and E is the dominance relation defined on V, is called dominator tree.

Let's take an example to show the CFG of a program and the corresponding dominator tree.

Put example code here:

```
void fun() {
  int iter, a, b;

  for (iter = 0; iter < 10; iter++) {
    a = 5;
    if (iter == a)
      b = 2;
    else
      b = 5;
  }
}
```

The CFG for the preceding code looks like the following:

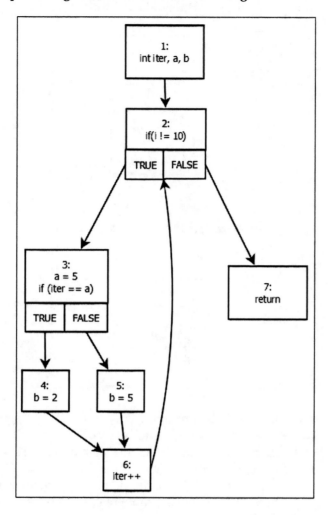

From what you have learned about dominance and dominator trees, the dominator tree for the preceding CFG looks something like the following:

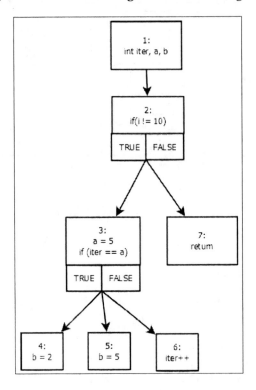

The first figure shows the CFG of the preceding code and the next figure shows the dominator tree for the same CFG. We have numbered each of the CFG components and we can see that 2 dominates 3 in the CFG, and 2 also dominates 4, 5, and 6. 3 dominates 4, 5, and 6 and is the immediate dominator of these. There is no dominance relation between 4 and 5. 6 is not dominated by 5 because there is another path available through 4 and for the same reasons, 4 does not dominate 6.

All the loop optimizations and transformation in LLVM are derived from the LoopPass class implemented in the LoopPass.cpp file located in lib/Analysis. The LPPassManager class is responsible for the handling of all LoopPasses.

The most important class to get started with loop processing is the LoopInfo Class, which is used to identify the natural loops in the code and to know the depth of various nodes in the CFG. Natural loops are the cyclic structures in a CFG. To define a natural loop in a CFG, we must know what a backedge is: it is an edge in the CFG where the source dominates the target. A natural loop can be defined by a backedge a->d that defines a subgraph of the CFG, where d is the header node and it contains all other basic blocks that can reach a without having to reach d.

We can see in the preceding diagram that the backedge `6->2` forms a natural loop consisting of the nodes `2`, `3`, `4`, `5`, and `6`.

The next important step is loop simplification that transforms the loop into a canonical form, which includes the insertion of a preheader to the loop, which in turn ensures that there is a single entry edge to the loop header from outside the loop. It also inserts loop exit blocks, which ensure that all exit blocks from the loop have predecessors only from within the loop. These insertion of pre-header and exit blocks help in later loop optimizations, such as Loop Independent Code Motion.

Loop Simplification also ensures that the loop will have only one backedge, that is if the loop header is having more than two predecessors, (from the pre header block and multiple latches to the loop) we adjust only this loop latch. One way of doing this is by inserting a new block which is the target of all the backedges and make this new block jump to loop header. Let's take a look at how a loop looks after **Loop Simplify Pass**. We will be able to see that a preheader node is inserted, new exit blocks are created, and there is only one backedge.

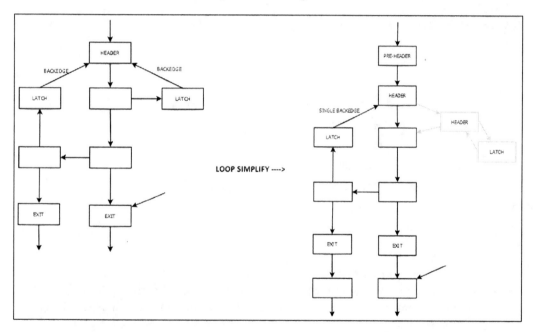

Now, after getting the required information from `LoopInfo` and simplifying the loop to a canonical form, we will look into some of the loop optimizations.

One of the main loop optimizations is **Loop Invariant Code Motion (LICM)** optimization. This pass tries to remove as much code from the body of the loop as possible. The condition for removal of the code is that this piece of code is invariant inside the loop, that is the output of this part of code not dependent on loop execution and it will remain same in every iteration of the loop. This is done by moving this piece of code either in the preheader block or moving the code to exit blocks. This pass is implemented in the `lib/TransformsScalar/LICM.cpp` file. If we look into the code of the loop, we see it requires `LoopInfo` and `LoopSimplify` passes to be run before it. Also, it needs the `AliasAnalysis` information. Alias analysis is needed to move loop invariant loads and calls out of the loop. If there is no load and call inside the loop that aliases anything stored, we can move these out of the loop. This also helps in scalar promotion of memory.

Let's look at an example to see how LICM is getting done.

Let's write the testcase in a file `licm.ll`:

```
$ cat licm.ll
define void @func(i32 %i) {
Entry:
        br label %Loop
Loop:
        %j = phi i32 [ 0, %Entry ], [ %Val, %Loop ]
        %loopinvar = mul i32 %i, 17
        %Val = add i32 %j, %loopinvar
        %cond = icmp eq i32 %Val, 0
        br i1 %cond, label %Exit, label %Loop
Exit:
        ret void
}
```

This `testcase` has a loop denoted by Loop block in the test code with the loop condition being `br i1 %cond, label %Exit, label %Loop` (Latch part of the loop). We can see the `%j` value, which is being used as the induction variable is derived after using the phi instruction. Basically, it tells to choose the value 0 if the control is coming from the Entry block and `%Val` if the control is coming from Loop block. In this, the invariant code can be seen as `%loopinvar = mul i32 %i, 17`, as `%loopinvar` value is independent of the iteration of loop and depends on the function argument only. So when we run the LICM pass, we expect this value to be hoisted out of the loop, thus preventing its computation in every iteration of the loop.

Let's run the `licm` pass and see the output:

```
$ opt -licm licm.ll -o licm.bc
$ llvm-dis licm.bc -o licm_opt.ll
$ cat licm_opt.ll
; ModuleID = 'licm.bc'

define void @func(i32 %i) {
Entry:
  %loopinvar = mul i32 %i, 17
  br label %Loop

Loop:
; preds = %Loop, %Entry
  %j = phi i32 [ 0, %Entry ], [ %Val, %Loop ]
  %Val = add i32 %j, %loopinvar
  %cond = icmp eq i32 %Val, 0
  br i1 %cond, label %Exit, label %Loop

Exit:
; preds = %Loop
  ret void
}
```

As we can see in the output, the calculation `%loopinvar = mul i32 %i, 17` is hoisted out of the loop, which is the expected output.

We have many other loop optimizations such as **Loop Rotation**, **Loop Interchange**, **Loop Unswitch**, and so on. The source codes for these can be looked under the LLVM folder `lib/Transforms/Scalar` to get more understanding about these optimizations. In the next section, we will see the concept of scalar evolution.

Scalar evolution

By scalar evolution, we mean how the value of a scalar changes in a program with the execution of code. We look at a particular scalar value and see how it is getting derived, what all other elements it is dependent on, whether this is known at compile time or not, and what all operations are being performed. We need to look into a block of code rather than looking into individual instructions. A scalar value is build up from two elements, a variable and an operation of constant step. The variable element that builds up this scalar value is unknown at compile time and its value can be known at run time only. The other element is the constant part. These elements themselves may be recursively broken into other elements such as a constant, an unknown value or an arithmetic operation.

The main idea here is to look at complete scalar value containing the unknown part at compile time and see how this value will evolve during execution and try to use this for optimization. One example is removing a redundant value for which the scalar evolution is similar to some other value in the same program.

In LLVM, we can use scalar evolution to analyze code that contains common integer arithmetic operations.

In LLVM `ScalarEvolution` class is implemented in `include/llvm/Analysis`, which is a LLVM pass and can be used analyze scalar expressions in a loop. It is able to recognize general induction variables (a variable in loop whose value is a function of loop iteration number) and represent them using object of SCEV class, which is used to represent analyzed expression in a program. Using this analysis trip count and other important analysis can be obtained. This scalar evolution analysis is mainly used in induction variable substitution and strength reduction of loops.

Let's take an example now and run the scalar evolution pass on it and see what output it generates.

Write a testcase `scalev1.ll` with a loop and some scalar values within the loop.

```
$ cat scalev1.ll
define void @fun() {
entry:
        br label %header
header:
        %i = phi i32 [ 1, %entry ], [ %i.next, %body ]
        %cond = icmp eq i32 %i, 10
        br i1 %cond, label %exit, label %body
body:
        %a = mul i32 %i, 5
        %b = or i32 %a, 1
        %i.next = add i32 %i, 1
        br label %header
exit:
        ret void
}
```

In this test case, we have a loop consisting of header and body blocks with %a and %b being the scalars in loop body of interest. Let's run the scalar evolution pass on this and see the output:

```
$ opt -analyze -scalar-evolution scalev1.ll
Printing analysis 'Scalar Evolution Analysis' for function 'fun':
Classifying expressions for: @fun
  %i = phi i32 [ 1, %entry ], [ %i.next, %body ]
  -->  {1,+,1}<%header> U: [1,11) S: [1,11)       Exits: 10
  %a = mul i32 %i, 5
  -->  {5,+,5}<%header> U: [5,51) S: [5,51)       Exits: 50
  %b = or i32 %a, 1
  -->  %b U: [1,0) S: full-set                    Exits: 51
  %i.next = add i32 %i, 1
  -->  {2,+,1}<%header> U: [2,12) S: [2,12)       Exits: 11
Determining loop execution counts for: @fun
Loop %header: backedge-taken count is 9
Loop %header: max backedge-taken count is 9
```

As we can see, the output of scalar evolution pass shows the range of values for a particular variable (U stands for unsigned range and S for signed range, here both are same) and the exit value, the value in that variable when the loop runs its last iteration. For example, the value %i has the range as [1,11), that is the starting iteration value is 1 and when the value of %i becomes 11 the condition %cond = icmp eq i32 %i, 10 becomes false and the loop breaks. So, the the value of %i when it exited the loop was 10, which is denoted by Exits: 10 in the output.

The value in the form of {x,+,y} representation, such as {2,+,1}, represents add recurrence, that is the expressions changing value during loop execution where x represents the base value at 0th iteration and y represents the value added to it on each subsequent iteration.

The output also shows the number of times the loop has iterated after the first run. Here, it shows the value 9 for backedge-taken, that is the loop has run 10 times in total. The max backedge-taken value is the least value which can never be less than the backedge-taken value, which here is 9.

This is the output for this example, you can try some other test cases and see what this pass outputs.

LLVM intrinsics

An intrinsic function is a function built in to the compiler. The compiler knows how to best implement the functionality in the most optimized way for these functions and replaces with a set of machine instruction for a particular backend. Often, the code for the function is inserted inline thus avoiding the overhead of function call (In many cases, we do call the library function. For example, for the functions listed in http://llvm.org/docs/LangRef.html#standard-c-library-intrinsics we make a call to libc). These are also called built-in functions for other compilers.

In LLVM these intrinsics are introduced during code optimization at IR level (Intrinsics written in program code can be emitted through frontend directly). These function names will start with a prefix "llvm.", which is a reserved word in LLVM. These functions are always external and a user cannot specify the body for these functions in his/her code. In our code, we can only call these intrinsic functions.

In this section, we will not go much deep into details. We will take an example and see how LLVM optimizes certain part of code with its own intrinsic functions.

Let's write a simple code:

```
$ cat intrinsic.cpp
int func()
{
        int a[5];

        for (int i = 0; i != 5; ++i)
                a[i] = 0;

        return a[0];
}
```

Now use Clang to generate the IR file. Using the command given below, we will get the intrinsic.ll file that contains the unoptimized IR without any intrinsic function.

```
$ clang -emit-llvm -S intrinsic.cpp
```

Now, use the opt tool to optimize the IR with O1 level of optimization.

```
$ opt -O1 intrinsic.ll -S -o -
; ModuleID = 'intrinsic.ll'
target datalayout = "e-m:e-i64:64-f80:128-n8:16:32:64-S128"
target triple = "x86_64-unknown-linux-gnu"


; Function Attrs: nounwind readnone uwtable
```

```
define i32 @_Z4funcv() #0 {
  %a = alloca [5 x i32], align 16
  %a2 = bitcast [5 x i32]* %a to i8*
  call void @llvm.memset.p0i8.i64(i8* %a2, i8 0, i64 20, i32 16, i1
false)
  %1 = getelementptr inbounds [5 x i32], [5 x i32]* %a, i64 0, i64 0
  %2 = load i32, i32* %1, align 16
  ret i32 %2
}


; Function Attrs: nounwind argmemonly
declare void @llvm.memset.p0i8.i64(i8* nocapture, i8, i64, i32, i1) #1
```

The important optimization to be noted here is the call to LLVM intrinsic function llvm.memset.p0i8.i64 to fill the array with value 0. The intrinsic functions may be used to implement vectorization and parallelization in the code, leading to better code generation. It might call the most optimized version of the memset call from the libc library and may choose to completely omit this function if there is no usage of this.

The first argument in the call specifies the array "a", that is the destination array where the value needs to be filled. The second argument specifies the value to be filled. The third argument to the call is specification about number of bytes to be filled. The fourth argument specifies the alignment of destination value. The last argument is to determine whether this is a volatile operation or not.

There is a list of such intrinsic functions in LLVM, a list of which can be found at http://llvm.org/docs/LangRef.html#intrinsic-functions.

Vectorization

Vectorization is an important optimization for compilers where we can vectorize code to execute an instruction on multiple datasets in one go. Advance target architecture typically have vector registers set and vector instructions—where broad range of data type (typically 128/246 bit) can be loaded into the vector registers and operations can be performed on those register set, performing two, four, and sometimes eight operations at the same time, with the cost of one scalar operation.

There are two types of vectorization in LLVM—**Superword-Level Parallelism (SLP)** and loop vectorization. Loop vectorization deals with vectorization opportunities in a loop, while SLP vectorization deals with vectorizing straight-line code in a basic block.

A vector instruction performs **Single-instruction multiple-data (SIMD)** operations; the same operation on multiple data lanes (in parallel).

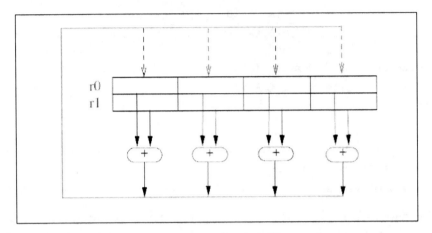

Let's look at how SLP Vectorization is implemented in LLVM infrastructure.

As the code itself attributes, the implementation of SLP Vectorization in LLVM is inspired by the work described in the paper *Loop-Aware SLP in GCC* by Ira Rosen, Dorit Nuzman, and Ayal Zaks. LLVM SLP Vectorization Pass implements the Bottom Up SLP vectorizer. It detects consecutive stores that can be put together into vector-stores. Next, it attempts to stores that can be put together into vector-stores. Next, it attempts to construct vectorizable tree using the use-def chains. If a profitable tree was found, the SLP vectorizer performs vectorization on the tree.

There are three stages to SLP Vectorization:

- Identify the pattern and determine if it is a valid Vectorization pattern
- Determine if it is profitable to vectorize the code
- If step 1 and 2 are true, then vectorize the code

Let's look at an example:

Consider addition of 4 consecutive elements of two arrays into third array.

```
int a[4], b[4], c[4];

void addsub() {
a[0] = b[0] + c[0];
a[1] = b[1] + c[1];
a[2] = b[2] + c[2];
a[3] = b[3] + c[3];
}
```

The IR for the preceding kind of expression will look like this:

```
; ModuleID = 'addsub.c'

@a = global [4 x i32] zeroinitializer, align 4
@b = global [4 x i32] zeroinitializer, align 4
@c = global [4 x i32] zeroinitializer, align 4

; Function Attrs: nounwind
define void @addsub() {
entry:
  %0 = load i32, i32* getelementptr inbounds ([4 x i32], [4 x i32]*
@b, i32 0, i32 0)
  %1 = load i32, i32* getelementptr inbounds ([4 x i32], [4 x i32]*
@c, i32 0, i32 0)
  %add = add nsw i32 %1, %0
  store i32 %add, i32* getelementptr inbounds ([4 x i32], [4 x i32]*
@a, i32 0, i32 0)
  %2 = load i32, i32* getelementptr inbounds ([4 x i32], [4 x i32]*
@b, i32 0, i32 1)
  %3 = load i32, i32* getelementptr inbounds ([4 x i32], [4 x i32]*
@c, i32 0, i32 1)
  %add1 = add nsw i32 %3, %2
  store i32 %add1, i32* getelementptr inbounds ([4 x i32], [4 x i32]*
@a, i32 0, i32 1)
  %4 = load i32, i32* getelementptr inbounds ([4 x i32], [4 x i32]*
@b, i32 0, i32 2)
  %5 = load i32, i32* getelementptr inbounds ([4 x i32], [4 x i32]*
@c, i32 0, i32 2)
  %add2 = add nsw i32 %5, %4
  store i32 %add2, i32* getelementptr inbounds ([4 x i32], [4 x i32]*
@a, i32 0, i32 2)
  %6 = load i32, i32* getelementptr inbounds ([4 x i32], [4 x i32]*
@b, i32 0, i32 3)
  %7 = load i32, i32* getelementptr inbounds ([4 x i32], [4 x i32]*
@c, i32 0, i32 3)
  %add3 = add nsw i32 %7, %6
  store i32 %add3, i32* getelementptr inbounds ([4 x i32], [4 x i32]*
@a, i32 0, i32 3)
  ret void
}
```

The expression tree for the preceding pattern can be visualized as a chain of stores and loads:

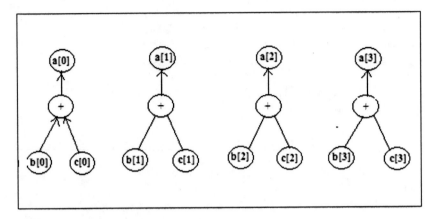

For the preceding expression tree, the bottom-up SLP Vectorization first constructs a chain that starts with a store instruction:

```
// Use the bottom up slp vectorizer to construct chains that start
// with store instructions.
 BoUpSLP R(&F, SE, TTI, TLI, AA, LI, DT, AC);
```

It then scans the tree already built in the preceding code for all the stores in the given basic block:

```
// Scan the blocks in the function in post order.
for (auto BB : post_order(&F.getEntryBlock())) {
  // Vectorize trees that end at stores.
  if (unsigned count = collectStores(BB, R)) {
    (void)count;
    DEBUG(dbgs() << "SLP: Found " << count << " stores to
vectorize.\n");
    Changed |= vectorizeStoreChains(R);
  }
  // Vectorize trees that end at reductions.
  Changed |= vectorizeChainsInBlock(BB, R);
}
```

The `collectStores()` function collects all the store references.

```
unsigned SLPVectorizer::collectStores(BasicBlock *BB, BoUpSLP &R) {
  unsigned count = 0;
  StoreRefs.clear();
  const DataLayout &DL = BB->getModule()->getDataLayout();
```

```
  for (Instruction &I : *BB) {
    StoreInst *SI = dyn_cast<StoreInst>(&I);
    if (!SI)
      continue;

    // Don't touch volatile stores.
    if (!SI->isSimple())
      continue;

    // Check that the pointer points to scalars.
    Type *Ty = SI->getValueOperand()->getType();
    if (!isValidElementType(Ty))
      continue;

    // Find the base pointer.
    Value *Ptr = GetUnderlyingObject(SI->getPointerOperand(), DL);

    // Save the store locations.
    StoreRefs[Ptr].push_back(SI);
    count++;
  }
  return count;
}
```

The function `SLPVectorizer::vectorizeStoreChains()` has three steps and function calls to each three steps:

```
bool SLPVectorizer::vectorizeStoreChain(ArrayRef<Value *> Chain,
                                        int CostThreshold, BoUpSLP &R,
                                        unsigned VecRegSize) {
  ...
  ...
    R.buildTree(Operands);

    int Cost = R.getTreeCost();

    DEBUG(dbgs() << "SLP: Found cost=" << Cost << " for VF=" << VF <<
"\n");
    if (Cost < CostThreshold) {
      DEBUG(dbgs() << "SLP: Decided to vectorize cost=" << Cost <<
"\n");
      R.vectorizeTree();
  ...
  ...
}
```

The first step is to identify pattern. The function `buildTree()` subsequently builds up the tree recursively as the preceding visualization.

```
void BoUpSLP::buildTree(ArrayRef<Value *> Roots,
                        ArrayRef<Value *> UserIgnoreLst) {
    ...

    ...

    buildTree_rec(Roots, 0);

    ...

    ...
}
```

For our given example, it will identify that all the store operations have binary addition operations as their operands:

```
void BoUpSLP::buildTree_rec(ArrayRef<Value *> VL, unsigned Depth) {
...

...

case Instruction::Add:
newTreeEntry(VL, true);
    DEBUG(dbgs() << "SLP: added a vector of bin op.\n");

    // Sort operands of the instructions so that each side is more
    // likely to have the sam opcode
    if (isa<BinaryOperator>(VL0) && VL0->isCommutative()) {
      ValueList Left, Right;
      reorderInputsAccordingToOpcode(VL, Left, Right);
      buildTree_rec(Left, Depth + 1);
      buildTree_rec(Right, Depth + 1);
      return;
    }
...

...
}
```

When the binary operation ADD is encountered, it again recursively builds tree (calling the same function) on LHS and RHS operands of the ADD operation, which in our case are both Load:

```
case Instruction::Load: {
    // Check that a vectorized load would load the same memory as a
    // scalar load.
    // For example we don't want vectorize loads that are smaller than
8 bit.
```

```
    // Even though we have a packed struct {<i2, i2, i2, i2>} LLVM
treats
    // loading/storing it as an i8 struct. If we vectorize loads/
stores from
    // such a struct we read/write packed bits disagreeing with the
    // unvectorized version.
    const DataLayout &DL = F->getParent()->getDataLayout();
    Type *ScalarTy = VL[0]->getType();

    if (DL.getTypeSizeInBits(ScalarTy) != DL.getTypeAllocSizeInBits(S
calarTy)) {
        BS.cancelScheduling(VL);
        newTreeEntry(VL, false);
        DEBUG(dbgs() << "SLP: Gathering loads of non-packed type.\n");
        return;
    }
    // Check if the loads are consecutive or of we need to swizzle
them.
    for (unsigned i = 0, e = VL.size() - 1; i < e; ++i) {
        LoadInst *L = cast<LoadInst>(VL[i]);
        if (!L->isSimple()) {
            BS.cancelScheduling(VL);
            newTreeEntry(VL, false);
            DEBUG(dbgs() << "SLP: Gathering non-simple loads.\n");
            return;
        }

        if (!isConsecutiveAccess(VL[i], VL[i + 1], DL)) {
            if (VL.size() == 2 && isConsecutiveAccess(VL[1], VL[0], DL)) {
                ++NumLoadsWantToChangeOrder;
            }
            BS.cancelScheduling(VL);
            newTreeEntry(VL, false);
            DEBUG(dbgs() << "SLP: Gathering non-consecutive loads.\n");
            return;
        }
    }
    ++NumLoadsWantToKeepOrder;
    newTreeEntry(VL, true);
    DEBUG(dbgs() << "SLP: added a vector of loads.\n");
    return;
}
```

While building the tree, there are several checks that validate if the tree can be vectorized. For example, in the preceding case, when loads are encountered across trees, it is checked whether they are consecutive loads or not. In our expression tree, the loads across trees in LHS—b[0], b[1], b[2], and b[3] are accessing consecutive memory location. Similarly, loads across tress in RHS—c[0], c[1], c[2] and c[3] are accessing consecutive memory location. If any of the checks fail for a given operation, the building of a tree is aborted and code is not vectorized.

After the pattern is identified and the vector tree is built, the next step is to get the cost of vectorizing the built tree. This effectively refers to the cost of the tree if it is vectorized compared to the cost of tree in current scalar form. If the vector cost is less than the scalar cost, it is beneficial to vectorize the tree:

```
int BoUpSLP::getTreeCost() {
  int Cost = 0;
  DEBUG(dbgs() << "SLP: Calculating cost for tree of size "
              << VectorizableTree.size() << ".\n");

  // We only vectorize tiny trees if it is fully vectorizable.
  if (VectorizableTree.size() < 3 && !isFullyVectorizableTinyTree()) {
    if (VectorizableTree.empty()) {
      assert(!ExternalUses.size() && "We should not have any external
users");
    }
    return INT_MAX;
  }

  unsigned BundleWidth = VectorizableTree[0].Scalars.size();

  for (unsigned i = 0, e = VectorizableTree.size(); i != e; ++i) {
    int C = getEntryCost(&VectorizableTree[i]);
    DEBUG(dbgs() << "SLP: Adding cost " << C << " for bundle that
starts with " << *VectorizableTree[i].Scalars[0] << " . \n" );
    Cost += C;
  }

  SmallSet<Value *, 16> ExtractCostCalculated;
  int ExtractCost = 0;
  for (UserList::iterator I = ExternalUses.begin(),
E = ExternalUses.end();
       I != E; ++I) {
    // We only add extract cost once for the same scalar.
```

```
        if (!ExtractCostCalculated.insert(I->Scalar).second)
          continue;

        // Uses by ephemeral values are free (because the ephemeral value
will be
        // removed prior to code generation, and so the extraction will be
        // removed as well).
        if (EphValues.count(I->User))
          continue;

        VectorType *VecTy = VectorType::get(I->Scalar->getType(),
BundleWidth);
        ExtractCost +=
            TTI->getVectorInstrCost(Instruction::ExtractElement, VecTy,
I->Lane);
    }

    Cost += getSpillCost();

    DEBUG(dbgs() << "SLP: Total Cost " << Cost + ExtractCost << ".\n");
    return Cost + ExtractCost;
}
```

An important interface to focus on here is the **TargetTransformInfo (TTI)**, which provides access to the codegen interfaces that are needed for IR-level transformations. In our SLP Vectorization, TTI is used to get the cost of the vector instruction of the built vector tree:

```
int BoUpSLP::getEntryCost(TreeEntry *E) {
...
...
case Instruction::Store: {
    // We know that we can merge the stores. Calculate the cost.
    int ScalarStCost = VecTy->getNumElements() *
                        TTI->getMemoryOpCost(Instruction::Store,
ScalarTy, 1, 0);
    int VecStCost = TTI->getMemoryOpCost(Instruction::Store,
VecTy, 1, 0);
    return VecStCost - ScalarStCost;
  }
...
...
}
```

In the same function, the cost of vector add is also calculated:

```
case Instruction::Add:  {
// Calculate the cost of this instruction.
    int ScalarCost = 0;
    int VecCost = 0;
    if (Opcode == Instruction::FCmp || Opcode == Instruction::ICmp ||
        Opcode == Instruction::Select) {
      VectorType *MaskTy = VectorType::get(Builder.getInt1Ty(),
VL.size());
      ScalarCost =
          VecTy->getNumElements() *
          TTI->getCmpSelInstrCost(Opcode, ScalarTy,
Builder.getInt1Ty());
      VecCost = TTI->getCmpSelInstrCost(Opcode, VecTy, MaskTy);
    } else {
      // Certain instructions can be cheaper to vectorize if they have
      // a constant second vector operand.
      TargetTransformInfo::OperandValueKind Op1VK =
          TargetTransformInfo::OK_AnyValue;
      TargetTransformInfo::OperandValueKind Op2VK =
          TargetTransformInfo::OK_UniformConstantValue;
      TargetTransformInfo::OperandValueProperties Op1VP =
          TargetTransformInfo::OP_None;
      TargetTransformInfo::OperandValueProperties Op2VP =
          TargetTransformInfo::OP_None;

      // If all operands are exactly the same ConstantInt then set the
      // operand kind to OK_UniformConstantValue.
      // If instead not all operands are constants, then set the
operand kind
      // to OK_AnyValue. If all operands are constants but not the
      // same, then set the operand kind to OK_NonUniformConstantValue.
      ConstantInt *CInt = nullptr;
      for (unsigned i = 0; i < VL.size(); ++i) {
        const Instruction *I = cast<Instruction>(VL[i]);
        if (!isa<ConstantInt>(I->getOperand(1))) {
          Op2VK = TargetTransformInfo::OK_AnyValue;
          break;
        }
        if (i == 0) {
          CInt = cast<ConstantInt>(I->getOperand(1));
```

```
            continue;
        }
        if (Op2VK == TargetTransformInfo::OK_UniformConstantValue &&
            CInt != cast<ConstantInt>(I->getOperand(1)))
          Op2VK = TargetTransformInfo::OK_NonUniformConstantValue;
      }
      // FIXME: Currently cost of model modification for division by
      // power of 2 is handled only for X86. Add support for other
      // targets.
      if (Op2VK == TargetTransformInfo::OK_UniformConstantValue &&
CInt &&
          CInt->getValue().isPowerOf2())
        Op2VP = TargetTransformInfo::OP_PowerOf2;

    ScalarCost = VecTy->getNumElements() *
                  TTI->getArithmeticInstrCost(Opcode, ScalarTy, Op1VK,
Op2VK, Op1VP, Op2VP);
      VecCost = TTI->getArithmeticInstrCost(Opcode, VecTy, Op1VK,
Op2VK, Op1VP, Op2VP);
    }
    return VecCost - ScalarCost;
  }
```

In our example, the total cost of the whole expression tree comes out to be `-12`, which indicates that it is profitable to vectorize the tree.

Finally, the tree is vectorized by the function call `R.vectorizeTree()` on the tree:

```
Value *BoUpSLP::vectorizeTree() {
  ...
  ...
  vectorizeTree(&VectorizableTree[0]);
  ...
  ...
}
```

Lets see all the steps the Vectorization process follows for our example. Note that this will require a 'Debug' build of the 'opt' tool.

```
$ opt -S -basicaa -slp-vectorizer -mtriple=aarch64-unknown-linuxgnu
-mcpu=cortex-a57 addsub.11 -debug
```

Features:

CPU:cortex-a57

SLP: Analyzing blocks in addsub.

SLP: Found 4 stores to vectorize.

SLP: Analyzing a store chain of length 4.

SLP: Analyzing a store chain of length 4

SLP: Analyzing 4 stores at offset 0

SLP: bundle: store i32 %add, i32* getelementptr inbounds ([4 x i32], [4 x i32]* @a, i32 0, i32 0)

SLP: initialize schedule region to   store i32 %add, i32* getelementptr inbounds ([4 x i32], [4 x i32]* @a, i32 0, i32 0)

SLP: extend schedule region end to   store i32 %add1, i32* getelementptr inbounds ([4 x i32], [4 x i32]* @a, i32 0, i32 1)

SLP: extend schedule region end to   store i32 %add2, i32* getelementptr inbounds ([4 x i32], [4 x i32]* @a, i32 0, i32 2)

SLP: extend schedule region end to   store i32 %add3, i32* getelementptr inbounds ([4 x i32], [4 x i32]* @a, i32 0, i32 3)

SLP: try schedule bundle [store i32 %add, i32* getelementptr inbounds ([4 x i32], [4 x i32]* @a, i32 0, i32 0); store i32 %add1, i32* getelementptr inbounds ([4 x i32], [4 x i32]* @a, i32 0, i32 1); store i32 %add2, i32* getelementptr inbounds ([4 x i32], [4 x i32]* @a, i32 0, i32 2); store i32 %add3, i32* getelementptr inbounds ([4 x i32], [4 x i32]* @a, i32 0, i32 3)] in block entry

SLP: update deps of [store i32 %add, i32* getelementptr inbounds ([4 x i32], [4 x i32]* @a, i32 0, i32 0); store i32 %add1, i32* getelementptr inbounds ([4 x i32], [4 x i32]* @a, i32 0, i32 1); store i32 %add2, i32* getelementptr inbounds ([4 x i32], [4 x i32]* @a, i32 0, i32 2); store i32 %add3, i32* getelementptr inbounds ([4 x i32], [4 x i32]* @a, i32 0, i32 3)]

SLP: update deps of /   store i32 %add1, i32* getelementptr inbounds ([4 x i32], [4 x i32]* @a, i32 0, i32 1)

SLP: update deps of /   store i32 %add2, i32* getelementptr inbounds ([4 x i32], [4 x i32]* @a, i32 0, i32 2)

SLP: update deps of /   store i32 %add3, i32* getelementptr inbounds ([4 x i32], [4 x i32]* @a, i32 0, i32 3)

SLP: gets ready on update: store i32 %add, i32* getelementptr inbounds ([4 x i32], [4 x i32]* @a, i32 0, i32 0)

SLP: We are able to schedule this bundle.

SLP: added a vector of stores.

SLP: bundle: %add = add nsw i32 %1, %0

SLP: extend schedule region start to   %add = add nsw i32 %1, %0

SLP: try schedule bundle [%add = add nsw i32 %1, %0; %add1 = add nsw i32 %3, %2; %add2 = add nsw i32 %5, %4; %add3 = add nsw i32 %7, %6] in block entry

SLP: update deps of [%add = add nsw i32 %1, %0; %add1 = add nsw i32 %3, %2; %add2 = add nsw i32 %5, %4; %add3 = add nsw i32 %7, %6]

SLP: update deps of / %add1 = add nsw i32 %3, %2

SLP: update deps of / %add2 = add nsw i32 %5, %4

SLP: update deps of / %add3 = add nsw i32 %7, %6

SLP: schedule [store i32 %add, i32* getelementptr inbounds ([4 x i32], [4 x i32]* @a, i32 0, i32 0); store i32 %add1, i32* getelementptr inbounds ([4 x i32], [4 x i32]* @a, i32 0, i32 1); store i32 %add2, i32* getelementptr inbounds ([4 x i32], [4 x i32]* @a, i32 0, i32 2); store i32 %add3, i32* getelementptr inbounds ([4 x i32], [4 x i32]* @a, i32 0, i32 3)]

SLP: gets ready (def): [%add = add nsw i32 %1, %0; %add1 = add nsw i32 %3, %2; %add2 = add nsw i32 %5, %4; %add3 = add nsw i32 %7, %6]

SLP: We are able to schedule this bundle.

SLP: added a vector of bin op.

SLP: bundle: %1 = load i32, i32* getelementptr inbounds ([4 x i32], [4 x i32]* @c, i32 0, i32 0)

SLP: extend schedule region start to %1 = load i32, i32* getelementptr inbounds ([4 x i32], [4 x i32]* @c, i32 0, i32 0)

SLP: try schedule bundle [%1 = load i32, i32* getelementptr inbounds ([4 x i32], [4 x i32]* @c, i32 0, i32 0); %3 = load i32, i32* getelementptr inbounds ([4 x i32], [4 x i32]* @c, i32 0, i32 1); %5 = load i32, i32* getelementptr inbounds ([4 x i32], [4 x i32]* @c, i32 0, i32 2); %7 = load i32, i32* getelementptr inbounds ([4 x i32], [4 x i32]* @c, i32 0, i32 3)] in block entry

SLP: update deps of [%1 = load i32, i32* getelementptr inbounds ([4 x i32], [4 x i32]* @c, i32 0, i32 0); %3 = load i32, i32* getelementptr inbounds ([4 x i32], [4 x i32]* @c, i32 0, i32 1); %5 = load i32, i32* getelementptr inbounds ([4 x i32], [4 x i32]* @c, i32 0, i32 2); %7 = load i32, i32* getelementptr inbounds ([4 x i32], [4 x i32]* @c, i32 0, i32 3)]

SLP: update deps of / %3 = load i32, i32* getelementptr inbounds ([4 x i32], [4 x i32]* @c, i32 0, i32 1)

SLP: update deps of / %5 = load i32, i32* getelementptr inbounds ([4 x i32], [4 x i32]* @c, i32 0, i32 2)

SLP: update deps of / %7 = load i32, i32* getelementptr inbounds ([4 x i32], [4 x i32]* @c, i32 0, i32 3)

SLP: schedule [%add = add nsw i32 %1, %0; %add1 = add nsw i32 %3, %2; %add2 = add nsw i32 %5, %4; %add3 = add nsw i32 %7, %6]

SLP: gets ready (def): [%1 = load i32, i32* getelementptr inbounds ([4 x i32], [4 x i32]* @c, i32 0, i32 0); %3 = load i32, i32* getelementptr inbounds ([4 x i32], [4 x i32]* @c, i32 0, i32 1); %5 = load i32, i32* getelementptr inbounds ([4 x i32], [4 x i32]* @c, i32 0, i32 2); %7 = load i32, i32* getelementptr inbounds ([4 x i32], [4 x i32]* @c, i32 0, i32 3)]

SLP: We are able to schedule this bundle.

SLP: added a vector of loads.

SLP: bundle: %0 = load i32, i32* getelementptr inbounds ([4 x i32], [4 x i32]* @b, i32 0, i32 0)

SLP: extend schedule region start to   %0 = load i32, i32* getelementptr inbounds ([4 x i32], [4 x i32]* @b, i32 0, i32 0)

SLP: try schedule bundle [%0 = load i32, i32* getelementptr inbounds ([4 x i32], [4 x i32]* @b, i32 0, i32 0); %2 = load i32, i32* getelementptr inbounds ([4 x i32], [4 x i32]* @b, i32 0, i32 1); %4 = load i32, i32* getelementptr inbounds ([4 x i32], [4 x i32]* @b, i32 0, i32 2); %6 = load i32, i32* getelementptr inbounds ([4 x i32], [4 x i32]* @b, i32 0, i32 3)] in block entry

SLP: update deps of [%0 = load i32, i32* getelementptr inbounds ([4 x i32], [4 x i32]* @b, i32 0, i32 0); %2 = load i32, i32* getelementptr inbounds ([4 x i32], [4 x i32]* @b, i32 0, i32 1); %4 = load i32, i32* getelementptr inbounds ([4 x i32], [4 x i32]* @b, i32 0, i32 2); %6 = load i32, i32* getelementptr inbounds ([4 x i32], [4 x i32]* @b, i32 0, i32 3)]

SLP: update deps of /   %2 = load i32, i32* getelementptr inbounds ([4 x i32], [4 x i32]* @b, i32 0, i32 1)

SLP: update deps of /   %4 = load i32, i32* getelementptr inbounds ([4 x i32], [4 x i32]* @b, i32 0, i32 2)

SLP: update deps of /   %6 = load i32, i32* getelementptr inbounds ([4 x i32], [4 x i32]* @b, i32 0, i32 3)

SLP: gets ready on update: %0 = load i32, i32* getelementptr inbounds ([4 x i32], [4 x i32]* @b, i32 0, i32 0)

SLP: We are able to schedule this bundle.

SLP: added a vector of loads.

SLP: Checking user: store i32 %add, i32* getelementptr inbounds ([4 x i32], [4 x i32]* @a, i32 0, i32 0).

SLP: Internal user will be removed: store i32 %add, i32* getelementptr inbounds ([4 x i32], [4 x i32]* @a, i32 0, i32 0).

SLP: Checking user: store i32 %add1, i32* getelementptr inbounds ([4 x i32], [4 x i32]* @a, i32 0, i32 1).

SLP: Internal user will be removed: store i32 %add1, i32* getelementptr inbounds ([4 x i32], [4 x i32]* @a, i32 0, i32 1).

SLP: Checking user: store i32 %add2, i32* getelementptr inbounds ([4 x i32], [4 x i32]* @a, i32 0, i32 2).

SLP: Internal user will be removed: store i32 %add2, i32* getelementptr inbounds ([4 x i32], [4 x i32]* @a, i32 0, i32 2).

SLP: Checking user: store i32 %add3, i32* getelementptr inbounds ([4 x i32], [4 x i32]* @a, i32 0, i32 3).

SLP: Internal user will be removed: store i32 %add3, i32* getelementptr inbounds ([4 x i32], [4 x i32]* @a, i32 0, i32 3).

SLP: Checking user: %add = add nsw i32 %1, %0.

SLP: Internal user will be removed: %add = add nsw i32 %1, %0.

SLP: Checking user: %add1 = add nsw i32 %3, %2.

SLP: Internal user will be removed: %add1 = add nsw i32 %3, %2.

SLP: Checking user: %add2 = add nsw i32 %5, %4.

SLP: Internal user will be removed: %add2 = add nsw i32 %5, %4.

SLP: Checking user: %add3 = add nsw i32 %7, %6.

SLP: Internal user will be removed: %add3 = add nsw i32 %7, %6.

SLP: Checking user: %add = add nsw i32 %1, %0.

SLP: Internal user will be removed: %add = add nsw i32 %1, %0.

SLP: Checking user: %add1 = add nsw i32 %3, %2.

SLP: Internal user will be removed: %add1 = add nsw i32 %3, %2.

SLP: Checking user: %add2 = add nsw i32 %5, %4.

SLP: Internal user will be removed: %add2 = add nsw i32 %5, %4.

SLP: Checking user: %add3 = add nsw i32 %7, %6.

SLP: Internal user will be removed: %add3 = add nsw i32 %7, %6.

SLP: Calculating cost for tree of size 4.

SLP: Adding cost -3 for bundle that starts with   store i32 %add, i32* getelementptr inbounds ([4 x i32], [4 x i32]* @a, i32 0, i32 0) .

SLP: Adding cost -3 for bundle that starts with   %add = add nsw i32 %1, %0 .

SLP: Adding cost -3 for bundle that starts with   %1 = load i32, i32* getelementptr inbounds ([4 x i32], [4 x i32]* @c, i32 0, i32 0) .

SLP: Adding cost -3 for bundle that starts with   %0 = load i32, i32* getelementptr inbounds ([4 x i32], [4 x i32]* @b, i32 0, i32 0) .

SLP: #LV: 0, Looking at   %add = add nsw i32 %1, %0

SLP: #LV: 1 add, Looking at   %1 = load i32, i32* getelementptr inbounds ([4 x i32], [4 x i32]* @c, i32 0, i32 0)

SLP: #LV: 2 , Looking at   %0 = load i32, i32* getelementptr inbounds ([4 x i32], [4 x i32]* @b, i32 0, i32 0)

```
SLP: SpillCost=0

SLP: Total Cost -12.

SLP: Found cost=-12 for VF=4

SLP: Decided to vectorize cost=-12

SLP: schedule block entry

SLP:    initially in ready list:   store i32 %add, i32* getelementptr
inbounds ([4 x i32], [4 x i32]* @a, i32 0, i32 0)

SLP:    schedule [ store i32 %add, i32* getelementptr inbounds ([4 x
i32], [4 x i32]* @a, i32 0, i32 0);  store i32 %add1, i32* getelementptr
inbounds ([4 x i32], [4 x i32]* @a, i32 0, i32 1);  store i32 %add2, i32*
getelementptr inbounds ([4 x i32], [4 x i32]* @a, i32 0, i32 2);  store
i32 %add3, i32* getelementptr inbounds ([4 x i32], [4 x i32]* @a, i32 0,
i32 3)]

SLP:    gets ready (def): [ %add = add nsw i32 %1, %0;  %add1 = add nsw
i32 %3, %2;  %add2 = add nsw i32 %5, %4;  %add3 = add nsw i32 %7, %6]

SLP:    schedule [ %add = add nsw i32 %1, %0;  %add1 = add nsw i32 %3,
%2;  %add2 = add nsw i32 %5, %4;  %add3 = add nsw i32 %7, %6]

SLP:    gets ready (def): [ %1 = load i32, i32* getelementptr inbounds
([4 x i32], [4 x i32]* @c, i32 0, i32 0);  %3 = load i32, i32*
getelementptr inbounds ([4 x i32], [4 x i32]* @c, i32 0, i32 1);  %5
= load i32, i32* getelementptr inbounds ([4 x i32], [4 x i32]* @c, i32
0, i32 2);  %7 = load i32, i32* getelementptr inbounds ([4 x i32], [4 x
i32]* @c, i32 0, i32 3)]

SLP:    gets ready (def): [ %0 = load i32, i32* getelementptr inbounds
([4 x i32], [4 x i32]* @b, i32 0, i32 0);  %2 = load i32, i32*
getelementptr inbounds ([4 x i32], [4 x i32]* @b, i32 0, i32 1);  %4
= load i32, i32* getelementptr inbounds ([4 x i32], [4 x i32]* @b, i32
0, i32 2);  %6 = load i32, i32* getelementptr inbounds ([4 x i32], [4 x
i32]* @b, i32 0, i32 3)]

SLP:    schedule [ %7 = load i32, i32* getelementptr inbounds ([4 x
i32], [4 x i32]* @c, i32 0, i32 0);  %6 = load i32, i32* getelementptr
inbounds ([4 x i32], [4 x i32]* @c, i32 0, i32 1);  %5 = load i32, i32*
getelementptr inbounds ([4 x i32], [4 x i32]* @c, i32 0, i32 2);  %4 =
load i32, i32* getelementptr inbounds ([4 x i32], [4 x i32]* @c, i32 0,
i32 3)]

SLP:    schedule [ %3 = load i32, i32* getelementptr inbounds ([4 x
i32], [4 x i32]* @b, i32 0, i32 0);  %2 = load i32, i32* getelementptr
inbounds ([4 x i32], [4 x i32]* @b, i32 0, i32 1);  %1 = load i32, i32*
getelementptr inbounds ([4 x i32], [4 x i32]* @b, i32 0, i32 2);  %0 =
load i32, i32* getelementptr inbounds ([4 x i32], [4 x i32]* @b, i32 0,
i32 3)]

SLP: Extracting 0 values .

SLP:    Erasing scalar: store i32 %add, i32* getelementptr inbounds ([4 x
i32], [4 x i32]* @a, i32 0, i32 0).
```

SLP: Erasing scalar: store i32 %add1, i32* getelementptr inbounds ([4 x i32], [4 x i32]* @a, i32 0, i32 1).

SLP: Erasing scalar: store i32 %add2, i32* getelementptr inbounds ([4 x i32], [4 x i32]* @a, i32 0, i32 2).

SLP: Erasing scalar: store i32 %add3, i32* getelementptr inbounds ([4 x i32], [4 x i32]* @a, i32 0, i32 3).

SLP: Erasing scalar: %add = add nsw i32 %8, %3.

SLP: Erasing scalar: %add1 = add nsw i32 %7, %2.

SLP: Erasing scalar: %add2 = add nsw i32 %6, %1.

SLP: Erasing scalar: %add3 = add nsw i32 %5, %0.

SLP: Erasing scalar: %8 = load i32, i32* getelementptr inbounds ([4 x i32], [4 x i32]* @c, i32 0, i32 0).

SLP: Erasing scalar: %7 = load i32, i32* getelementptr inbounds ([4 x i32], [4 x i32]* @c, i32 0, i32 1).

SLP: Erasing scalar: %6 = load i32, i32* getelementptr inbounds ([4 x i32], [4 x i32]* @c, i32 0, i32 2).

SLP: Erasing scalar: %5 = load i32, i32* getelementptr inbounds ([4 x i32], [4 x i32]* @c, i32 0, i32 3).

SLP: Erasing scalar: %3 = load i32, i32* getelementptr inbounds ([4 x i32], [4 x i32]* @b, i32 0, i32 0).

SLP: Erasing scalar: %2 = load i32, i32* getelementptr inbounds ([4 x i32], [4 x i32]* @b, i32 0, i32 1).

SLP: Erasing scalar: %1 = load i32, i32* getelementptr inbounds ([4 x i32], [4 x i32]* @b, i32 0, i32 2).

SLP: Erasing scalar: %0 = load i32, i32* getelementptr inbounds ([4 x i32], [4 x i32]* @b, i32 0, i32 3).

SLP: Optimizing 0 gather sequences instructions.

SLP: vectorized "addsub"

The final vectorized output is:

```
; ModuleID = 'addsub.ll'
target triple = "aarch64-unknown-linuxgnu"


@a = global [4 x i32] zeroinitializer, align 4
@b = global [4 x i32] zeroinitializer, align 4
@c = global [4 x i32] zeroinitializer, align 4


define void @addsub()  {
entry:
```

```
  %0 = load <4 x i32>, <4 x i32>* bitcast ([4 x i32]* @b to <4 x i32>*),
align 4

  %1 = load <4 x i32>, <4 x i32>* bitcast ([4 x i32]* @c to <4 x i32>*),
align 4

  %2 = add nsw <4 x i32> %1, %0

  store <4 x i32> %2, <4 x i32>* bitcast ([4 x i32]* @a to <4 x i32>*),
align 4

  ret void
}
```

Summary

In this chapter, we concluded the optimizer part of the compiler where we had seen block level optimizations. We took the examples of loop optimization, Scalar Evolution, Vectorization, and LLVM Intrinsic functions. We also saw how SLP Vectorization is handled in LLVM. However, there are many other such optimizations that you can look into and get a hold of.

In the next chapter, we will see how this IR is converted to **Directed Acyclic Graph**. We have some optimizations at selectionDAG level as well, which we will take a look at.

6

IR to Selection DAG phase

Until the previous chapter, we saw how a frontend language can be converted to LLVM IR. We also saw how IR can be transformed into more optimized code. After a series of analysis and transformation passes, the final IR is the most optimized machine independent code. However, the IR is still an abstract representation of the actual machine code. The compiler has to generate target architecture code for execution.

LLVM uses DAG — a directed acyclic graph representation for code generation. The idea is to convert IR into a SelectionDAG and then go over a series of phases — DAG combine, legalization, instruction selection, instruction scheduling, etc — to finally allocate registers and emit machine code. Note that register allocation and instruction scheduling take place in an intertwined manner.

We are going to cover following topics in this chapter:

- Converting IR to selectionDAG
- Legalizing selectionDAG
- Optimizing selectionDAG
- Instruction selection
- Scheduling and emitting machine instructions
- Register allocation
- Code emission

Converting IR to selectionDAG

An IR instruction can be represented by an SDAG node. The whole set of instructions thus forms an interconnected directed acyclic graph, with each node corresponding to an IR instruction.

For example, consider the following LLVM IR:

```
$ cat test.ll
define i32 @test(i32 %a, i32 %b, i32 %c) {
%add = add nsw i32 %a, %b
%div = sdiv i32 %add, %c
ret i32 %div
}
```

LLVM provides a `SelectionDAGBuilder` interface to create DAG nodes corresponding to IR instructions. Consider the binary operation:

```
%add = add nsw i32 %a, %b
```

The following function is called when the given IR is encountered:

```
void SelectionDAGBuilder::visit(unsigned Opcode, const User &I) {
  // Note: this doesn't use InstVisitor, because it has to work with
  // ConstantExpr's in addition to instructions.
  switch (Opcode) {
  default: llvm_unreachable("Unknown instruction type encountered!");
    // Build the switch statement using the Instruction.def file.
#define HANDLE_INST(NUM, OPCODE, CLASS) \
    case Instruction::OPCODE: visit##OPCODE((const CLASS&)I); break;
#include "llvm/IR/Instruction.def"
  }
}
```

Depending on the opcode—which is `Add` here—the corresponding visit function is invoked. In this case, `visitAdd()` is invoked, which further invokes the `visitBinary()` function. The `visitBinary()` function is as follows:

```
void SelectionDAGBuilder::visitBinary(const User &I, unsigned OpCode)
{
  SDValue Op1 = getValue(I.getOperand(0));
  SDValue Op2 = getValue(I.getOperand(1));

  bool nuw = false;
  bool nsw = false;
```

```
    bool exact = false;
    FastMathFlags FMF;

    if (const OverflowingBinaryOperator *OFBinOp =
            dyn_cast<const OverflowingBinaryOperator>(&I)) {
      nuw = OFBinOp->hasNoUnsignedWrap();
      nsw = OFBinOp->hasNoSignedWrap();
    }
    if (const PossiblyExactOperator *ExactOp =
            dyn_cast<const PossiblyExactOperator>(&I))
      exact = ExactOp->isExact();
    if (const FPMathOperator *FPOp = dyn_cast<const FPMathOperator>(&I))
      FMF = FPOp->getFastMathFlags();

    SDNodeFlags Flags;
    Flags.setExact(exact);
    Flags.setNoSignedWrap(nsw);
    Flags.setNoUnsignedWrap(nuw);
    if (EnableFMFInDAG) {
      Flags.setAllowReciprocal(FMF.allowReciprocal());
      Flags.setNoInfs(FMF.noInfs());
      Flags.setNoNaNs(FMF.noNaNs());
      Flags.setNoSignedZeros(FMF.noSignedZeros());
      Flags.setUnsafeAlgebra(FMF.unsafeAlgebra());
    }
    SDValue BinNodeValue = DAG.getNode(OpCode, getCurSDLoc(),
    Op1.getValueType(), Op1, Op2, &Flags);
    setValue(&I, BinNodeValue);
  }
```

This function takes two operands of the binary operator from IR and stores them into `SDValue` type. Then it invokes the `DAG.getNode()` function with opcode of the binary operator. This results in formation of a DAG node, which somewhat looks like the following:

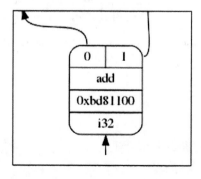

The operands `0` and `1` are load DAG nodes.

Consider the IR:

```
%div = sdiv i32 %add, %c
```

On encountering the `sdiv` instruction, the function `visitSDiv()` is invoked.

```
void SelectionDAGBuilder::visitSDiv(const User &I) {
  SDValue Op1 = getValue(I.getOperand(0));
  SDValue Op2 = getValue(I.getOperand(1));

  SDNodeFlags Flags;
  Flags.setExact(isa<PossiblyExactOperator>(&I) &&
              cast<PossiblyExactOperator>(&I)->isExact());
  setValue(&I, DAG.getNode(ISD::SDIV, getCurSDLoc(),
  Op1.getValueType(), Op1, Op2, &Flags));
}
```

Similar to `visitBinary()`, this function also stores the two operands into `SDValue` gets a DAG node with `ISD::SDIV` as its operator. The node looks like the following:

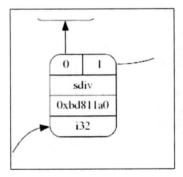

In our IR, the operand 0 is `%add`. Operand 1 is `%c`, which is passed as an argument to the function, which transforms to a load node when converting IR to `SelectionDAG`. For implementation of Load DAG node, go through the `visitLoad()` function in the `lib/CodeGen/SelectionDAG/SelectionDAGBuilder.cpp` file.

After visiting all the IR instructions mentioned earlier, finally the IR is converted to `SelectionDAG` as follows:

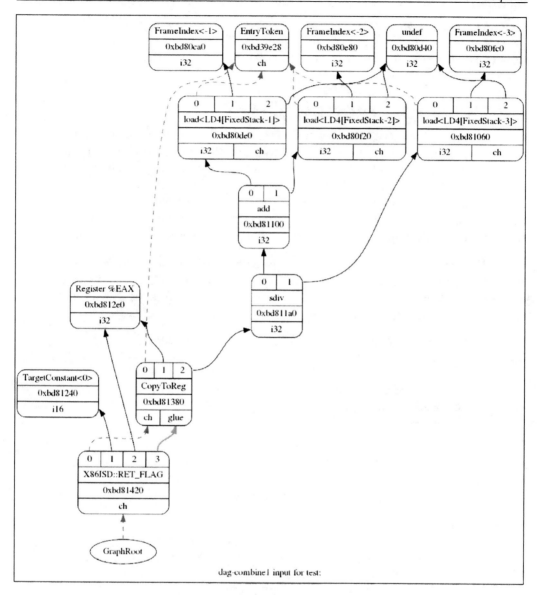

In the preceding diagram, note the following:

- Black arrows mean data flow dependency
- Red arrows mean glue dependency
- Blue dashed arrows mean chain dependency

Glue prevents the two nodes from being broken up during scheduling. Chain dependencies prevent nodes with side effects. A data dependency indicates when an instruction depends on the result of a previous instruction.

Legalizing SelectionDAG

In the preceding topic, we saw how an IR is converted to SelectionDAG. The whole process didn't involve any knowledge of target architecture for which we are trying to generate code. A DAG node might be illegal for the given target architecture. For example, the X86 architecture doesn't support the sdiv instruction. Instead, it supports sdivrem instruction. This target specific information is conveyed to the SelectionDAG phase by the TargetLowering interface. Targets implement this interface to describe how LLVM IR instructions should be lowered to legal SelectionDAG operations.

In our IR case, we need to 'expand' the sdiv instruction to 'sdivrem' instruction. In the function void SelectionDAGLegalize::LegalizeOp(SDNode *Node), the TargetLowering::Expand case is encountered, which invokes the ExpandNode() function call on that particular node.

```
void SelectionDAGLegalize::LegalizeOp(SDNode *Node){
...

...
case TargetLowering::Expand:
    ExpandNode(Node);
    return;
...

...
}
```

This function expands SDIV into the SDIVREM node:

```
case ISD::SDIV: {
    bool isSigned = Node->getOpcode() == ISD::SDIV;
    unsigned DivRemOpc = isSigned ? ISD::SDIVREM : ISD::UDIVREM;
    EVT VT = Node->getValueType(0);
    SDVTList VTs = DAG.getVTList(VT, VT);
    if (TLI.isOperationLegalOrCustom(DivRemOpc, VT) ||
        (isDivRemLibcallAvailable(Node, isSigned, TLI) &&
        useDivRem(Node, isSigned, true)))
      Tmp1 = DAG.getNode(DivRemOpc, dl, VTs, Node->getOperand(0),
                         Node->getOperand(1));
    else if (isSigned)
```

```
        Tmp1 = ExpandIntLibCall(Node, true,
                                RTLIB::SDIV_I8,
                                RTLIB::SDIV_I16, RTLIB::SDIV_I32,
                                RTLIB::SDIV_I64, RTLIB::SDIV_I128);
      else
        Tmp1 = ExpandIntLibCall(Node, false,
                                RTLIB::UDIV_I8,
                                RTLIB::UDIV_I16, RTLIB::UDIV_I32,
                                RTLIB::UDIV_I64, RTLIB::UDIV_I128);
      Results.push_back(Tmp1);
      break;
    }
```

Finally, after legalization, the node becomes `ISD::SDIVREM`:

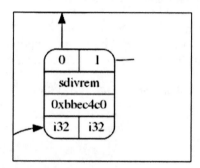

Thus the above instruction has been 'legalized' mapping to the instruction supported on the target architecture. What we saw above was an example of expand legalization. There are two other types of legalization—promotion and custom. A promotion promotes one type to a larger type. A custom legalization involves target-specific hook (maybe a custom operation—majorly seen with IR intrinsic). We leave it to the readers to explore these more in the CodeGen phase.

Optimizing SelectionDAG

After converting the IR into SelectionDAG, many opportunities may arise to optimize the DAG itself. These optimization takes place in the DAGCombiner phase. These opportunities may arise due to set of architecture specific instructions.

Let's take an example:

```
#include <arm_neon.h>
unsigned hadd(uint32x4_t a) {
  return a[0] + a[1] + a[2] + a[3];
}
```

The preceding example in IR looks like the following:

```
define i32 @hadd(<4 x i32> %a) nounwind {
  %vecext = extractelement <4 x i32> %a, i32 3
  %vecext1 = extractelement <4 x i32> %a, i32 2
  %add = add i32 %vecext, %vecext1
  %vecext2 = extractelement <4 x i32> %a, i32 1
  %add3 = add i32 %add, %vecext2
  %vecext4 = extractelement <4 x i32> %a, i32 0
  %add5 = add i32 %add3, %vecext4
  ret i32 %add5
}
```

The example is basically extracting single element from a vector of `<4xi32>` and adding each element of the vector to give a scalar result.

Advanced architectures such as ARM has one single instruction to do the preceding operation—adding across single vector. The SDAG needs to be combined into a single DAG node by identifying the preceding pattern in `SelectionDAG`.

This can be done while selecting instruction in `AArch64DAGToDAGISel`.

```
SDNode *AArch64DAGToDAGISel::Select(SDNode *Node) {
...

...

  case ISD::ADD: {
    if (SDNode *I = SelectMLAV64LaneV128(Node))
      return I;
    if (SDNode *I = SelectADDV(Node))
      return I;
    break;
  }
}
```

We define the `SelectADDV()` function as follows:

```
SDNode *AArch64DAGToDAGISel::SelectADDV(SDNode *N) {
  if (N->getValueType(0) != MVT::i32)
    return nullptr;
  SDValue SecondAdd;
  SDValue FirstExtr;
  if (!checkVectorElemAdd(N, SecondAdd, FirstExtr))
    return nullptr;

  SDValue Vector = FirstExtr.getOperand(0);
  if (Vector.getValueType() != MVT::v4i32)
```

```
      return nullptr;

   uint64_t LaneMask = 0;
   ConstantSDNode *LaneNode = cast<ConstantSDNode>(FirstExtr-
>getOperand(1));
   LaneMask |= 1 << LaneNode->getZExtValue();

   SDValue ThirdAdd;
   SDValue SecondExtr;
   if (!checkVectorElemAdd(SecondAdd.getNode(), ThirdAdd, SecondExtr))
      return nullptr;
   if (Vector != SecondExtr.getOperand(0))
      return nullptr;
   ConstantSDNode *LaneNode2 = cast<ConstantSDNode>(SecondExtr-
>getOperand(1));
   LaneMask |= 1 << LaneNode2->getZExtValue();
   SDValue LHS = ThirdAdd.getOperand(0);
   SDValue RHS = ThirdAdd.getOperand(1);
   if (LHS.getOpcode() != ISD::EXTRACT_VECTOR_ELT ||
       RHS.getOpcode() != ISD::EXTRACT_VECTOR_ELT ||
       LHS.getOperand(0) != Vector ||
       RHS.getOperand(0) != Vector)
      return nullptr;
   ConstantSDNode *LaneNode3 = cast<ConstantSDNode>(LHS-
>getOperand(1));
   LaneMask |= 1 << LaneNode3->getZExtValue();
   ConstantSDNode *LaneNode4 = cast<ConstantSDNode>(RHS-
>getOperand(1));
   LaneMask |= 1 << LaneNode4->getZExtValue();
   if (LaneMask != 0x0F)
      return nullptr;
   return CurDAG->getMachineNode(AArch64::ADDVv4i32v, SDLoc(N),
MVT::i32,
                                 Vector);
}
```

Note that we have defined a helper function `checkVectorElemAdd()` earlier to check the chain of add selection DAG nodes.

```
   static bool checkVectorElemAdd(SDNode *N, SDValue &Add, SDValue &Extr)
   {
     SDValue Op0 = N->getOperand(0);
     SDValue Op1 = N->getOperand(1);
     const unsigned Opc0 = Op0->getOpcode();
```

```
    const unsigned Opc1 = Op1->getOpcode();

    const bool AddLeft  = (Opc0 == ISD::ADD && Opc1 == ISD::EXTRACT_
VECTOR_ELT);
    const bool AddRight = (Opc0 == ISD::EXTRACT_VECTOR_ELT && Opc1 ==
ISD::ADD);

  if (!(AddLeft || AddRight))
    return false;

  Add  = AddLeft ? Op0 : Op1;
  Extr = AddLeft ? Op1 : Op0;
  return true;
}
```

Let's see how this affects the code generation:

```
$ llc -mtriple=aarch64-linux-gnu -verify-machineinstrs hadd.ll
```

Before the preceding code, the final code generated will be as follows:

```
mov   w8, v0.s[3]
mov   w9, v0.s[2]
add   w8, w8, w9
mov   w9, v0.s[1]
add   w8, w8, w9
fmov  w9, s0
add   w0, w8, w9
ret
```

Clearly, the preceding code is a scalar code. After adding the preceding patch and compiling, the code generated will be as follows:

```
addv  s0, v0.4s
fmov  w0, s0
ret
```

Instruction Selection

The `SelectionDAG` at this phase is optimized and legalized. However, the instructions are still not in machine code form. These instructions need to be mapped to architecture-specific instructions in the `SelectionDAG` itself. The `TableGen` class helps select target-specific instructions.

The `CodeGenAndEmitDAG()` function calls the `DoInstructionSelection()` function that visits each DAG node and calls the Select() function for each node. The `Select()` function is the main hook targets implement to select a node. The `Select()` function is a virtual method to be implemented by the targets.

For consideration, assume our target architecture is X86. The `X86DAGToDAGISel::Select()` function intercepts some nodes for manual matching, but delegates the bulk of the work to the `X86DAGToDAGISel::SelectCode()` function. The `X86DAGToDAGISel::SelectCode()` function is auto generated by `TableGen`. It contains the matcher table, followed by a call to the generic `SelectionDAGISel::SelectCodeCommon()` function, passing it the table.

```
SDNode *ResNode = SelectCode(Node);
```

For example, consider the following:

```
$ cat test.ll
define i32 @test(i32 %a, i32 %b, i32 %c) {
%add = add nsw i32 %a, %b
%div = sdiv i32 %add, %c
ret i32 %div
}
```

Before instruction selection, the SDAG looks like the following:

```
$ llc –view-isel-dags test.ll
```

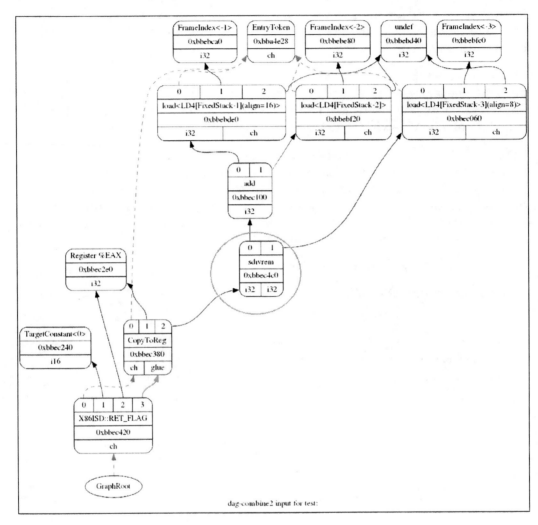

After Instruction Selection, SDAG looks like the following:

```
$ llc -view-sched-dags test.ll
```

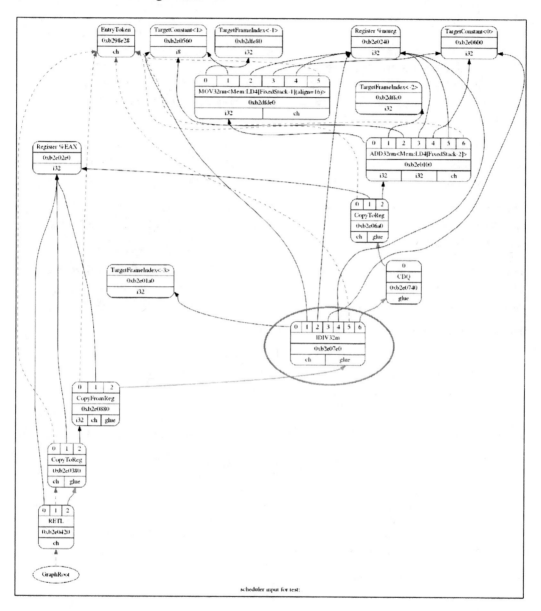

Scheduling and emitting machine instructions

Until now, we have been performing the operations on DAG. Now, for the machine to execute, we need to convert the DAGs into instruction that the machine can execute. One step towards it is emitting the list of instructions into `MachineBasicBlock`. This is done by the `Scheduler`, whose goal is to linearize the DAGs. The scheduling is dependent on the target architecture, as certain Targets will have target specific hooks which can affect the scheduling.

The class `InstrEmitter::EmitMachineNode` takes `SDNode *Node` as one of the input parameters for which it will be emitting machine instructions of the class `MachineInstr`. These instructions are emitted into a `MachineBasicBlock`.

The function calls `EmitSubregNode`, `EmitCopyToRegClassNode` and `EmitRegSequence` for the handling of `subreg` insert/extract, `COPY_TO_REGCLASS`, and `REG_SEQUENCE` respectively.

The call `MachineInstrBuilder MIB = BuildMI(*MF, Node->getDebugLoc(), II);` is used to build the Machine Instruction. The `CreateVirtualRegisters` function is called to add result register values created by this instruction.

The `for` loop emits the operands of the instruction :

```
for (unsigned i = NumSkip; i != NodeOperands; ++i)
    AddOperand(MIB, Node->getOperand(i), i-NumSkip+NumDefs, &II,
               VRBaseMap, /*IsDebug=*/false, IsClone, IsCloned);
MBB->insert(InsertPos, MIB);
```

It inserts the instruction into its position in the `MachineBasicBlock`.

The following code marks unused registers as dead:

```
if (!UsedRegs.empty() || II.getImplicitDefs())
    MIB->setPhysRegsDeadExcept(UsedRegs, *TRI);
```

As we had discussed earlier that the target specific hooks affect the scheduling, the code for that in this function is as follows:

```
if (II.hasPostISelHook())
    TLI->AdjustInstrPostInstrSelection(MIB, Node);
```

The `AdjustInstrPostInstrSelection` is a virtual function implemented by Targets.

Let's take an example to see the machine instructions generated in this step. To do this, we need to pass the command-line option -print-machineinstrs to the llc tool. Let's take the same testcode used earlier:

```
$ cat test.ll
define i32 @test(i32 %a, i32 %b, i32 %c) {
%add = add nsw i32 %a, %b
%div = sdiv i32 %add, %c
ret i32 %div
}
```

Now, invoke the llc command and pass the -print-machineinstrs to it. Pass test.ll as the input file and store the output in the outfile:

```
llc -print-machineinstrs test.ll > outfile 2>&1
```

The outfile is large, containing many other phases of code generation apart from scheduling. We need to look into the section after "# After Instruction Selection:" in the output file, which is as follows:

```
    # After Instruction Selection:
    # Machine code for function test: SSA
    Function Live Ins: %EDI in %vreg0, %ESI in %vreg1, %EDX in %vreg2
    BB#0: derived from LLVM BB %0
        Live Ins: %EDI %ESI %EDX
            %vreg2<def> = COPY %EDX; GR32:%vreg2
            %vreg1<def> = COPY %ESI; GR32:%vreg1
            %vreg0<def> = COPY %EDI; GR32:%vreg0
            %vreg3<def,tied1> = ADD32rr %vreg0<tied0>, %vreg1,
    %EFLAGS<imp-def,dead>; GR32:%vreg3,%vreg0,%vreg1
            %EAX<def> = COPY %vreg3; GR32:%vreg3
            CDQ %EAX<imp-def>, %EDX<imp-def>, %EAX<imp-use>
            IDIV32r %vreg2, %EAX<imp-def>, %EDX<imp-def,dead>,
    %EFLAGS<imp-def,dead>, %EAX<imp-use>, %EDX<imp-use>; GR32:%vreg2
            %vreg4<def> = COPY %EAX; GR32:%vreg4
            %EAX<def> = COPY %vreg4; GR32:%vreg4
            RETQ %EAX
    # End machine code for function test.
```

We can see in the output that certain places being taken by physical registers and some by virtual registers. We can also see the machine instruction IDIV32r in the output. In the next section, we will see how physical registers are assigned to these virtual registers present in the code.

Register allocation

The next step of the code generator is register allocation. As we saw in the previous example, some of the registers being used were virtual registers. Register allocation is the task of assigning physical registers to these virtual registers. In LLVM, the virtual registers can be infinite in number, but the numbers of physical registers are limited depending on the target. So, by register allocation, we aim at maximizing the number of physical registers being assigned to virtual registers. We must note that the physical registers are limited in number, so it is not always possible that all the virtual registers can be assigned a physical register. If there is no physical register available at some point and we need a physical register for a variable, we might move a variable that is present in physical register to main memory and thus assign the freed register to the variable we want. This process of moving a variable from physical register to memory is called **spilling**. There are various algorithms to calculate which variable should be spilled from register to memory.

Another important role that the register allocator plays is SSA form deconstruction. The phi instructions present in the machine instruction till now need to be replaced with a regular instruction. The traditional way of doing so is to replace it with a copy instruction.

It must be noted that some of the machine fragments have already registers assigned to them. This is due to target requirements where it wants certain registers fixed to certain operations. Apart from these fixed registers, the register allocator takes care of the rest of the non-fixed registers.

Register allocation for mapping virtual registers to physical registers can be done in the following two ways:

- **Direct Mapping**: It makes use of the TargetRegisterInfo class and the MachineOperand class. The developer in this case needs to provide the location where load and store instructions are to be inserted to get values from the memory and store values in the memory.
- **Indirect Mapping**: In this, the VirtRegMap class takes care of inserting loads and stores. It also gets value from memory and stores value to memory. We need to use the VirtRegMap::assignVirt2Phys(vreg, preg) function for mapping virtual register to physical register.

LLVM has four register allocation techniques. We will briefly look what they are without going into the details of the algorithm. The four allocators are as follows:

- **Basic Register Allocator**: The most basic register allocation technique of all the techniques. It can serve as a starter for implementing other register allocation techniques. The algorithm makes use of spill weight for prioritizing the virtual registers. The virtual register with the least weight gets the register allocated to it. When no physical register is available, the virtual register is spilled to memory.

- **Fast Register Allocator**: This allocation is done at basic block level at a time and attempts to reuse values in registers by keeping them in registers for longer period of time.

- **PBQP Register Allocator**: As mentioned in the source code file for this register allocation(llvm/lib/CodeGen/RegAllocPBQP.cpp), this allocator works by representing the register allocator as a PBQP problem and then solving it using PBQP solver.

- **Greedy Register Allocator**: This is one of the efficient allocator of LLVM and works across the functions. Its allocation is done using live range splitting and minimizing spill costs.

Let's take an example to see the register allocation for the previous testcode test.ll and see how vregs are replaced with actual registers. Let's take the greedy allocator for allocation. You can choose any other allocator as well. The target machine used is x86-64 machine.

```
$ llc test.ll -regalloc=greedy -o test1.s
$ cat test1.s
  .text
  .file   "test.ll"
  .globl  test
  .align  16, 0x90
  .type   test,@function
test:                                   # @test
  .cfi_startproc
# BB#0:
  movl   %edx, %ecx
  leal   (%rdi,%rsi), %eax
  cltd
  idivl  %ecx
  retq
.Lfunc_end0:
  .size   test, .Lfunc_end0-test
  .cfi_endproc
  .section  ".note.GNU-stack","",@progbits
```

We can see all the vregs present are gone now and have been replaced by actual registers. The machine used here was x86-64. You can try out register allocation with pbqp allocator and see the difference in allocation. The leal (%rdi,%rsi), %eax instruction will be replaced with the following instructions:

```
movl    %esi, %edx
movl    %edi, %eax
leal    (%rax, %rdx), %eax.
```

Code Emission

We started from LLVM IR in the first section and converted it to SelectioDAG and then to MachineInstr. Now, we need to emit this code. Currently, we have LLVM JIT and MC to do so. LLVM JIT is the traditional way of generating the object code for a target on the go directly in the memory. What we are more interested in is the LLVM MC layer.

The MC layer is responsible for generation of assembly file/object file from the MachineInstr passed on to it from the previous step. In the MC Layer, the instructions are represented as MCInst, which are lightweight, as in they don't carry much information about the program as MachineInstr.

The code emission starts with the AsmPrinter class, which is overloaded by the target specific AsmPrinter class. This class deals with general lowering process by converting the MachineFunction functions into MC label constructs by making use of the target specific MCInstLowering interface(for x86 it is X86MCInstLower class in the lib/Target/x86/X86MCInstLower.cpp file).

Now, we have MCInst instructions that are passed to MCStreamer class for further step of generating either the assembly file or object code. Depending on the choice MCStreamer makes use of its subclass MCAsmStreamer to generate assembly code and MCObjectStreamer to generate the object code.

The target specific MCInstPrinter is called by MCAsmStreamer to print the assembly instructions. To generate the binary code, the LLVM object code assembler is called by MCObjectStreamer. The assembler in turn calls the MCCodeEmitter::EncodeInstruction() to generate the binary instructions.

We must note that the MC Layer is one of the big difference between LLVM and GCC. GCC always outputs assembly and then needs an external assembler to transform this assembly into object files, whereas for LLVM using its own assembler we can easily print the instructions in binary and by putting some wraps around them can generate the object file directly. This not only guarantees that the output emitted in text or binary forms will be same but also saves time over GCC by removing the calls to external processes.

Now, let's take an example to look at the MC Instruction corresponding to assembly using the llc tool. We make use of the same testcode test.ll file used earlier in the chapter.

To view the MC Instructions, we need to pass the command-line option -asm-show-inst option to llc. It will show the MC instructions as assembly file comments.

```
llc test.ll -asm-show-inst -o -
  .text
  .file    "test.ll"
  .globl   test
  .align   16, 0x90
  .type    test,@function
test:                                    # @test
  .cfi_startproc
# BB#0:
  movl  %edx, %ecx                # <MCInst #1674 MOV32rr
                                  #   <MCOperand Reg:22>
                                  #   <MCOperand Reg:24>>

  leal   (%rdi,%rsi), %eax        # <MCInst #1282 LEA64_32r
                                  #   <MCOperand Reg:19>
                                  #   <MCOperand Reg:39>
                                  #   <MCOperand Imm:1>
                                  #   <MCOperand Reg:43>
                                  #   <MCOperand Imm:0>
                                  #   <MCOperand Reg:0>>
  cltd                           # <MCInst #388 CDQ>
  idivl  %ecx                     # <MCInst #903 IDIV32r
                                  #   <MCOperand Reg:22>>

  retq                           # <MCInst #2465 RETQ
                                  #   <MCOperand Reg:19>>
.Lfunc_end0:
  .size    test, .Lfunc_end0-test
  .cfi_endproc


  .section   ".note.GNU-stack","",@progbits
```

We see the MCInst and MCOperands in the assembly comments. We can also view the binary encoding in assembly comments by passing the option -show-mc-encoding to llc.

```
$ llc test.ll -show-mc-encoding -o -
  .text
  .file   "test.ll"
  .globl   test
  .align   16, 0x90
  .type    test,@function
test:                                       # @test
  .cfi_startproc
# BB#0:
  movl    %edx, %ecx              # encoding: [0x89,0xd1]
  leal    (%rdi,%rsi), %eax       # encoding: [0x8d,0x04,0x37]
  cltd                             # encoding: [0x99]
  idivl   %ecx                    # encoding: [0xf7,0xf9]
  retq                             # encoding: [0xc3]
.Lfunc_end0:
  .size   test, .Lfunc_end0-test
  .cfi_endproc

  .section  ".note.GNU-stack","",@progbits
```

Summary

In this chapter, we saw how LLVM IR is converted to SelectionDAG. The SDAG then goes through variety of transformation. The instructions are legalized, so are the data types. SelectionDAG also goes through the optimization phase where DAG nodes are combined to result in optimal nodes, which may be target-spacific. After DAG combine, it goes through instruction selection phase, where target architecture instructions are mapped to DAG nodes. After this, the DAGs are ordered in a linear order to facilitate execution by CPU, these DAGs are converted to MachineInstr and DAGs are destroyed. Assigning of physical register takes place in the next step to all the virtual registers present in the code. After this, the MC layer comes into picture and deals with the generation of Object and Assembly Code. Going ahead in the next chapter, we will see how to define a target; the various aspects of how a target is represented in LLVM by making use of Table Descriptor files and TableGen.

7
Generating Code for Target Architecture

The code generated by the compiler finally has to execute on the target machines. The abstract form of the LLVM IR helps to generate code for various architectures. The target machine can be anything – CPU, GPU, DSP's, and so on. The target machine has some defining aspects such as the register sets, the instruction set, the calling convention of the function, and the instruction pipeline. These aspects or properties are generated using the **tablegen** tool so that they can be used easily while programming code generation for the machine.

LLVM has a pipeline structure for the backend, where instructions travel through phases—from the LLVM IR to **SelectionDAG**, then to **MachineDAG**, then to **MachineInstr**, and finally to **MCInst**. The IR is converted to SelectionDAG. SelectionDAG then goes through legalization and optimizations. After this stage, the DAG nodes are mapped to target instructions (instruction selection). The DAG then goes through instruction scheduling, emitting linear sequences of instructions. The virtual registers are then allotted the target machine registers, which involves optimal register allocation minimizing memory spills.

This chapter describes how to represent target architecture. It also describes how to emit assembly code.

The topics discussed in this chapter are as follows:

- Defining registers and register sets
- Defining the calling convention
- Defining the instruction set
- Implementing frame lowering

- Selecting an instruction
- Printing an instruction
- Registering a target

Sample backend

To understand target code generation, we define a simple RISC-type architecture TOY machine with minimal registers, say r0-r3, a stack pointer SP, a link register, LR (for storing the return address); and a CPSR – current state program register. The calling convention of this TOY backend is similar to the ARM thumb-like architecture—arguments passed to the function will be stored in register sets r0-r1, and the return value will be stored in r0.

Defining registers and register sets

Register sets are defined using the tablegen tool. Tablegen helps to maintain large number of records of domain specific information. It factors out the common features of these records. This helps in reducing duplication in the description and forms a structural way of representing domain information. Please visit http://llvm.org/docs/TableGen/ to understand tablegen in detail. TableGen files are interpreted by the TableGen binary: llvm-tblgen.

We have described our sample backend in the preceding paragraph, which has four registers (r0-r3), a stack register (SP), and a link register (LR). These can be specified in the TOYRegisterInfo.td file. The tablegen function provides the Register class, which can be extended to specify the registers. Create a new file named TOYRegisterInfo.td.

The registers can be defined by extending the Register class.

```
class TOYReg<bits<16> Enc, string n> : Register<n> {
let HWEncoding = Enc;
let Namespace = "TOY";
}
```

The registers r0-r3 belong to a general purpose Register class. This can be specified by extending RegisterClass.

```
foreach i = 0-3 in {
def R#i : R<i, "r"#i >;
}

def GRRegs : RegisterClass<"TOY", [i32], 32,
(add R0, R1, R2, R3, SP)>;
```

The remainings, register SP, LR, and CPSR, can be defined as follows:

```
def SP : TOYReg<13, "sp">;
def LR : TOYReg<14, "lr">;
def CPSR  : TOYReg<16, "cpsr">;
```

When the whole thing is put together, the TOYRegisterInfo.td looks like the following:

```
class TOYReg<bits<16> Enc, string n> : Register<n> {
let HWEncoding = Enc;
let Namespace = "TOY";
}


foreach i = 0-3 in {
def R#i : R<i, "r"#i >;
}


def SP : TOYReg<13, "sp">;
def LR : TOYReg<14, "lr">;
def GRRegs : RegisterClass<"TOY", [i32], 32,
(add R0, R1, R2, R3, SP)>;
```

We can put this file in a new folder named TOY in the parent folder named Target in the llvm's root directory, which is llvm_root_directory/lib/Target/TOY/TOYRegisterInfo.td

The tablegen tool llvm-tablegen, processes this .td file to generate the .inc file, which generally has enums generated for these registers. These enums can be used in the .cpp files, in which the registers can be referenced as TOY::R0.

Defining the calling convention

The calling convention specifies how values are passed to and returned from a function call. Our TOY architecture specifies that two arguments are passed in two registers, r0 and r1, while the remaining ones are passed to the stack. Calling convention defined is then used in the Instruction Selection phase by referring to the function pointer.

While defining a calling convention, we have to represent two sections—one to define the convention return value, and other to define the convention for argument passing. The parent class CallingConv is inherited to define the calling convention.

In our TOY architecture, the return value is stored in r0 register. If there are more arguments, integer values get stored in stack slots that are 4 bytes in size and 4-byte aligned. This can be declared in TOYCallingConv.td as follows:

```
def RetCC_TOY : CallingConv<[
CCIfType<[i32], CCAssignToReg<[R0]>>,
CCIfType<[i32], CCAssignToStack<4, 4>>
]>;
```

The argument passing convention can be defined as follows:

```
def CC_TOY : CallingConv<[
CCIfType<[i8, i16], CCPromoteToType<i32>>,
CCIfType<[i32], CCAssignToReg<[R0, R1]>>,
CCIfType<[i32], CCAssignToStack<4, 4>>
]>;
```

The preceding declaration says three things, which are as follows:

- If the datatype of the arguments is i8 or i16, it will get promoted to i32
- The first two arguments will be stored in register r0 and r1
- If there are more arguments, they will be stored in stack

We also define the callee-saved register since callee-saved registers are used to hold long-lived values that should be preserved across calls.

```
def CC_Save : CalleeSavedRegs<(add R2, R3)>;
```

The llvm-tablegen tool generates a TOYCallingConv.inc file after building the project, which will be included in the Instruction Selection phase in the TOYISelLowering.cpp file.

Defining the instruction set

Architectures have rich instruction sets to represent various operations supported by the target machine. Typically, three things need to be defined in the target description file when representing the instructions:

- operands
- the assembly string
- the instruction pattern

The specification contains a list of definitions or outputs, and a list of uses or inputs. There can be different operand classes, such as the Register class, and the immediate and more complex register+imm operands.

For example, we define register to register addition for our Toy machine as follows in `TOYInstrInfo.td`:

```
def ADDrr : InstTOY<(outs GRRegs:$dst),
(ins GRRegs:$src1, GRRegs:$src2),
"add $dst, $src1,z$src2",
[(set i32:$dst, (add i32:$src1, i32:$src2))]>;
```

In the above declaration, the 'ins' has two registers $src1 and $src2 belonging to the general purpose register class, which holds the two operands. The result of the operation will be put into 'outs', which is a $dst register belonging to the general purpose `Register` class. The assembly string is "add $dst, $src1,z$src2". The values of $src1, $src2 and $dst will be determined at the time of register allocation. So, an assembly will be generated for add between two registers, like this:

```
add r0, r0, r1
```

We saw above how a simple instruction can be represented using tablegen. Similar to the `add register to register` instruction, a `subtract register from a register` instruction can be defined. We leave it to the readers to try it out. A more detailed representation of complex instructions can be examined from the ARM or X86 architecture specifications in the project code.

Implementing frame lowering

Frame lowering involves emitting function prologue and epilogue. The prologue happens at the beginning of a function. It sets up the stack frame of the called function. The epilogue happens last in a function, it restores the stack frame of the calling (parent) function.

The "stack" serves several purposes in the execution of a program, as follows:

- Keeping track of return address, when calling a function
- Storage of local variables in the context of a function call
- Passing arguments from the caller to the callee.

Thus there are 2 main functions that need to be defined when implementing frame lowering – `emitPrologue()` and `emitEpilogue()`.

The `emitPrologue()` function can be defined as follows:

```
void TOYFrameLowering::emitPrologue(MachineFunction &MF) const {
    const TargetInstrInfo &TII = *MF.getSubtarget().getInstrInfo();
    MachineBasicBlock &MBB = MF.front();
```

```
    MachineBasicBlock::iterator MBBI = MBB.begin();

    uint64_t StackSize = computeStackSize(MF);
    if (!StackSize) {
      return;
    }
    unsigned StackReg = TOY::SP;
    unsigned OffsetReg = materializeOffset(MF, MBB, MBBI, (unsigned)
StackSize);
    if (OffsetReg) {
      BuildMI(MBB, MBBI, dl, TII.get(TOY::SUBrr), StackReg)
          .addReg(StackReg)
          .addReg(OffsetReg)
          .setMIFlag(MachineInstr::FrameSetup);
    } else {
      BuildMI(MBB, MBBI, dl, TII.get(TOY::SUBri), StackReg)
          .addReg(StackReg)
          .addImm(StackSize)
          .setMIFlag(MachineInstr::FrameSetup);
    }
  }
```

The above function moves over **Machine Basic Block**. It calculates stack size for the function, calculates offset for the stack size, and emits instructions to set up the frame with a stack register.

Similarly, the `emitEpilogue()` function can be defined as follows:

```
    void TOYFrameLowering::emitEpilogue(MachineFunction &MF,
                                        MachineBasicBlock &MBB) const {
      const TargetInstrInfo &TII = *MF.getSubtarget().getInstrInfo();
      MachineBasicBlock::iterator MBBI = MBB.getLastNonDebugInstr();
      DebugLoc dl = MBBI->getDebugLoc();
      uint64_t StackSize = computeStackSize(MF);
      if (!StackSize) {
        return;
      }
      unsigned StackReg = TOY::SP;
      unsigned OffsetReg = materializeOffset(MF, MBB, MBBI, (unsigned)
StackSize);
      if (OffsetReg) {
        BuildMI(MBB, MBBI, dl, TII.get(TOY::ADDrr), StackReg)
            .addReg(StackReg)
            .addReg(OffsetReg)
            .setMIFlag(MachineInstr::FrameSetup);
```

```
    } else {
      BuildMI(MBB, MBBI, dl, TII.get(TOY::ADDri), StackReg)
          .addReg(StackReg)
          .addImm(StackSize)
          .setMIFlag(MachineInstr::FrameSetup);
    }
}
```

The preceding function also calculates stack size, over goes the machine basic block, and sets up the function frame when returning from the function. Please note that the stack here is descending.

The emitPrologue() function first computes the stack size to determine whether the prologue is required at all. Then it adjusts the stack pointer by calculating the offset. For the emitEpilogue(), it first checks whether the epilogue is required or not. Then it restores the stack pointer to what it was at the beginning of the function.

For example, consider this input IR:

```
%p = alloca i32, align 4
store i32 2, i32* %p
%b = load i32* %p, align 4
%c = add nsw i32 %a, %b
```

The TOY assembly generated will look like this:

```
sub sp, sp, #4 ; prologue
movw r1, #2
str r1, [sp]
add r0, r0, #2
add sp, sp, #4 ; epilogue
```

Lowering instructions

In this chapter, we will see the implementation of 3 things – Function call calling convention, Formal argument calling convention, and Return value calling convention. We create a file TOYISelLowering.cpp, and implement Instructions Lowering in it.

First, let's look at how a call calling convention can be implemented.

```
SDValue TOYTar-getLoweing::LowerCall(TargetLowering::CallLoweringInfo
&CLI, SmallVectorImpl<SDValue> &InVals)
 const {
  SelectionDAG &DAG = CLI.DAG;
  SDLoc &Loc = CLI.DL;
```

```
SmallVectorImpl<ISD::OutputArg> &Outs = CLI.Outs;
SmallVectorImpl<SDValue> &OutVals = CLI.OutVals;
SmallVectorImpl<ISD::InputArg> &Ins = CLI.Ins;
SDValue Chain = CLI.Chain;
SDValue Callee = CLI.Callee;
CallingConv::ID CallConv = CLI.CallConv;
const bool isVarArg = CLI.IsVarArg;

CLI.IsTailCall = false;

if (isVarArg) {
  llvm_unreachable("Unimplemented");
}

// Analyze operands of the call, assigning locations to each
// operand.
SmallVector<CCValAssign, 16> ArgLocs;
CCState CCInfo(CallConv, isVarArg, DAG.getMachineFunction(),
ArgLocs, *DAG.getContext());
CCInfo.AnalyzeCallOperands(Outs, CC_TOY);

// Get the size of the outgoing arguments stack space
// requirement.
const unsigned NumBytes = CCInfo.getNextStackOffset();

Chain = DAG.getCALLSEQ_START(Chain,
                             DAG.getIntPtrConstant(NumBytes, Loc,
true), Loc);

SmallVector<std::pair<unsigned, SDValue>, 8> RegsToPass;
SmallVector<SDValue, 8> MemOpChains;

// Walk the register/memloc assignments, inserting copies/loads.
for (unsigned i = 0, e = ArgLocs.size(); i != e; ++i) {
  CCValAssign &VA = ArgLocs[i];
  SDValue Arg = OutVals[i];

  // We only handle fully promoted arguments.
  assert(VA.getLocInfo() == CCValAssign::Full && "Unhandled loc
  info");

  if (VA.isRegLoc()) {
    RegsToPass.push_back(std::make_pair(VA.getLocReg(), Arg));
    continue;
  }
```

```
    assert(VA.isMemLoc() &&
           "Only support passing arguments through registers or
           via the stack");

    SDValue StackPtr = DAG.getRegister(TOY::SP, MVT::i32);
    SDValue PtrOff = DAG.getIntPtrConstant(VA.getLocMemOffset(),
    Loc);
    PtrOff = DAG.getNode(ISD::ADD, Loc, MVT::i32, StackPtr,
    PtrOff);
    MemOpChains.push_back(DAG.getStore(Chain, Loc, Arg, PtrOff,
                                       MachinePointerInfo(), false,
false, 0));
  }


  // Emit all stores, make sure they occur before the call.
  if (!MemOpChains.empty()) {
    Chain = DAG.getNode(ISD::TokenFactor, Loc, MVT::Other,
MemOpChains);
  }


  // Build a sequence of copy-to-reg nodes chained together with
  // token chain
  // and flag operands which copy the outgoing args into the
  // appropriate regs.
  SDValue InFlag;
  for (auto &Reg : RegsToPass) {
    Chain = DAG.getCopyToReg(Chain, Loc, Reg.first, Reg.second,
InFlag);
    InFlag = Chain.getValue(1);
  }


  // We only support calling global addresses.
  GlobalAddressSDNode *G = dyn_cast<GlobalAddressSDNode>(Callee);
  assert(G && "We only support the calling of global address-es");

  EVT PtrVT = getPointerTy(DAG.getDataLayout());
  Callee = DAG.getGlobalAddress(G->getGlobal(), Loc, PtrVT, 0);

  std::vector<SDValue> Ops;
  Ops.push_back(Chain);
  Ops.push_back(Callee);

  // Add argument registers to the end of the list so that they
  // are known live into the call.
  for (auto &Reg : RegsToPass) {
```

```
      Ops.push_back(DAG.getRegister(Reg.first, Reg.second.
getValueType()));
  }

  // Add a register mask operand representing the call-preserved
  // registers.
  const uint32_t *Mask;
  const TargetRegisterInfo *TRI = DAG.getSubtarget().
getRegisterInfo();
  Mask = TRI->getCallPreservedMask(DAG.getMachineFunction(),
CallConv);

  assert(Mask && "Missing call preserved mask for calling
  convention");
  Ops.push_back(DAG.getRegisterMask(Mask));

  if (InFlag.getNode()) {
    Ops.push_back(InFlag);
  }

  SDVTList NodeTys = DAG.getVTList(MVT::Other, MVT::Glue);

  // Returns a chain and a flag for retval copy to use.
  Chain = DAG.getNode(TOYISD::CALL, Loc, NodeTys, Ops);
  InFlag = Chain.getValue(1);

  Chain = DAG.getCALLSEQ_END(Chain, DAG.getIntPtrConstant(NumBytes,
Loc, true),
                                    DAG.getIntPtrConstant(0, Loc, true),
InFlag, Loc);
  if (!Ins.empty()) {
    InFlag = Chain.getValue(1);
  }

  // Handle result values, copying them out of physregs into vregs
  // that we return.
  return LowerCallResult(Chain, InFlag, CallConv, isVarArg, Ins,
                         Loc, DAG, InVals);
}
```

In the above function, we first analyzed the operands of the call, assigned a location to each operand, and calculated the size of the argument stack space. Then we scanned the `register/memloc` assignment and inserted `copies` and `loads`. For our sample target, we support passing arguments through registers or via stack (remember the calling convention defined in the previous section). We then emit all the stores making sure they happen before call. We build a sequence of `copy-to-reg` nodes that copy the outgoing arguments into the appropriate registers. Then, we add a register mask operand representing the call-preserved registers. We return a chain and a flag for return value copy to use and finally handle result values, copying them out of `physregs` into `vregs` that we return.

We will now look at the implementation of a formal argument calling convention.

```
SDValue TOYTargetLowering::LowerFormalArguments(
    SDValue Chain, CallingConv::ID CallConv, bool isVarArg,
    const SmallVectorImpl<ISD::InputArg> &Ins, SDLoc dl, SelectionDAG
&DAG,
    SmallVectorImpl<SDValue> &InVals) const {
  MachineFunction &MF = DAG.getMachineFunction();
  MachineRegisterInfo &RegInfo = MF.getRegInfo();

  assert(!isVarArg && "VarArg not supported");

  // Assign locations to all of the incoming arguments.
  SmallVector<CCValAssign, 16> ArgLocs;
  CCState CCInfo(CallConv, isVarArg, DAG.getMachineFunction(),
  ArgLocs, *DAG.getContext());

  CCInfo.AnalyzeFormalArguments(Ins, CC_TOY);

  for (auto &VA : ArgLocs) {
    if (VA.isRegLoc()) {
      // Arguments passed in registers
      EVT RegVT = VA.getLocVT();
      assert(RegVT.getSimpleVT().SimpleTy == MVT::i32 &&
             "Only support MVT::i32 register passing");
      const unsigned VReg =
          RegInfo.createVirtualRegister(&TOY::GRRegsRegClass);
      RegInfo.addLiveIn(VA.getLocReg(), VReg);
      SDValue ArgIn = DAG.getCopyFromReg(Chain, dl, VReg, RegVT);

      InVals.push_back(ArgIn);
      continue;
    }
```

```
    assert(VA.isMemLoc() &&
           "Can only pass arguments as either registers or via the
           stack");

    const unsigned Offset = VA.getLocMemOffset();

    const int FI = MF.getFrameInfo()->CreateFixedObject(4, Offset,
    true);
    EVT PtrTy = getPointerTy(DAG.getDataLayout());
    SDValue FIPtr = DAG.getFrameIndex(FI, PtrTy);

    assert(VA.getValVT() == MVT::i32 &&
           "Only support passing arguments as i32");
    SDValue Load = DAG.getLoad(VA.getValVT(), dl, Chain, FIPtr,
                              MachinePointerInfo(), false, false,
    false, 0);

    InVals.push_back(Load);
  }
  return Chain;
}
```

In the above implementation of a formal argument calling convention, we assigned a location to all the incoming arguments. We handle only the arguments passed via a register or a stack. We will now look at the implementation of a return value calling convention.

```
bool TOYTargetLowering::CanLowerReturn(
    CallingConv::ID CallConv, MachineFunction &MF, bool isVarArg,
    const SmallVectorImpl<ISD::OutputArg> &Outs, LLVMContext &Context)
const {
  SmallVector<CCValAssign, 16> RVLocs;
  CCState CCInfo(CallConv, isVarArg, MF, RVLocs, Context);
  if (!CCInfo.CheckReturn(Outs, RetCC_TOY)) {
    return false;
  }
  if (CCInfo.getNextStackOffset() != 0 && isVarArg) {
    return false;
  }
  return true;
}
```

```
SDValue
TOYTargetLowering::LowerReturn(SDValue Chain, CallingConv::ID
CallConv, bool isVarArg, const SmallVec torImpl<ISD::OutputArg>
& Outs, const SmallVectorImpl<SDValue> const SmallVec
torImpl<ISD::OutputArg> & Outs,
  if (isVarArg) {
    report_fatal_error("VarArg not supported");
  }

  // CCValAssign - represent the assignment of
  // the return value to a location
  SmallVector<CCValAssign, 16> RVLocs;

  // CCState - Info about the registers and stack slot.
  CCState CCInfo(CallConv, isVarArg, DAG.getMachineFunction(), RVLocs,
                *DAG.getContext());

  CCInfo.AnalyzeReturn(Outs, RetCC_TOY);

  SDValue Flag;
  SmallVector<SDValue, 4> RetOps(1, Chain);

  // Copy the result values into the output registers.
  for (unsigned i = 0, e = RVLocs.size(); i < e; ++i) {
    CCValAssign &VA = RVLocs[i];
    assert(VA.isRegLoc() && "Can only return in registers!");

    Chain = DAG.getCopyToReg(Chain, dl, VA.getLocReg(), OutVals[i],
Flag);

    Flag = Chain.getValue(1);
    RetOps.push_back(DAG.getRegister(VA.getLocReg(), VA.getLocVT()));
  }

  RetOps[0] = Chain; // Update chain.

  // Add the flag if we have it.
  if (Flag.getNode()) {
    RetOps.push_back(Flag);
  }

  return DAG.getNode(TOYISD::RET_FLAG, dl, MVT::Other, RetOps);
}
```

We first see if we can lower a return. We then gather information about registers and stack slots. We copy the result values in the output registers and finally return a DAG node for a return value.

Printing an instruction

Printing an assembly instruction is an important step in generating target code. Various classes are defined that work as a gateway to the streamers.

First, we initialize the class for instruction, assigning the operands, the assembly string, pattern, the output variable, and so on in the TOYInstrFormats.td file:

```
class InstTOY<dag outs, dag ins, string asmstr, list<dag> pattern>
    : Instruction {
  field bits<32> Inst;
  let Namespace = "TOY";
  dag OutOperandList = outs;
  dag InOperandList = ins;
  let AsmString = asmstr;
  let Pattern = pattern;
  let Size = 4;
}
```

Then, we define functions to print operands in TOYInstPrinter.cpp.

```
void TOYInstPrinter::printOperand(const MCInst *MI, unsigned OpNo,
                                  raw_ostream &O) {
  const MCOperand &Op = MI->getOperand(OpNo);
  if (Op.isReg()) {
    printRegName(O, Op.getReg());
    return;
  }
  if (Op.isImm()) {
    O << "#" << Op.getImm();
    return;
  }
  assert(Op.isExpr() && "unknown operand kind in printOperand");
  printExpr(Op.getExpr(), O);
}
```

This function simply prints operands, registers, or immediate values, as the case may be.

We also define a function to print the register names in the same file:

```
void TOYInstPrinter::printRegName(raw_ostream &OS, unsigned RegNo)
const {
  OS << StringRef(getRegisterName(RegNo)).lower();
}
```

Next, we define a function to print the instruction:

```
void TOYInstPrinter::printInst(const MCInst *MI, raw_ostream &O,
                               StringRef Annot) {
  printInstruction(MI, O);
  printAnnotation(O, Annot);
}
```

Next, we declare and define assembly info as follows:

We create a `TOYMCAsmInfo.h` and declare an `ASMInfo` class:

```
#ifndef TOYTARGETASMINFO_H
#define TOYTARGETASMINFO_H
#include "llvm/MC/MCAsmInfoELF.h"
namespace llvm {
class StringRef;
class Target;
class TOYMCAsmInfo : public MCAsmInfoELF {
  virtual void anchor();

public:
  explicit TOYMCAsmInfo(StringRef TT);
};
} // namespace llvm
#endif
```

The constructor can be defined in `TOYMCAsmInfo.cpp` as follows:

```
#include "TOYMCAsmInfo.h"
#include "llvm/ADT/StringRef.h"
using namespace llvm;
void TOYMCAsmInfo::anchor() {}
TOYMCAsmInfo::TOYMCAsmInfo(StringRef TT) {
  SupportsDebugInformation = true;
  Data16bitsDirective = "\t.short\t";
  Data32bitsDirective = "\t.long\t";
  Data64bitsDirective = 0;
  ZeroDirective = "\t.space\t";
  CommentString = "#";
```

```
    AscizDirective = ".asciiz";
    HiddenVisibilityAttr = MCSA_Invalid;
    HiddenDeclarationVisibilityAttr = MCSA_Invalid;
    ProtectedVisibilityAttr = MCSA_Invalid;
}
```

For compilation, we define `LLVMBuild.txt` as follows:

```
[component_0]
type = Library
name = TOYAsmPrinter
parent = TOY
required_libraries = MC Support
add_to_library_groups = TOY
```

Furthermore, we define the `CMakeLists.txt` file as follows:

```
add_llvm_library(LLVMTOYAsmPrinter
TOYInstPrinter.cpp
)
```

When the final compilation takes place, the `llc` tool — a static compiler — will generate the assembly of the TOY architecture (after registering the TOY architecture with the `llc` tool).

To register our TOY target with static compiler `llc`, follow the steps mentioned below:

1. First, add the entry of the TOY backend to `llvm_root_dir/CMakeLists.txt`:

```
set(LLVM_ALL_TARGETS
AArch64
ARM
...
...
TOY
)
```

2. Then, add the `toy` entry to `llvm_root_dir/include/llvm/ADT/Triple.h`:

```
class Triple {
public:
enum ArchType {
UnknownArch,
arm, // ARM (little endian): arm, armv.*, xscale
armeb, // ARM (big endian): armeb
aarch64, // AArch64 (little endian): aarch64
...
...
toy // TOY: toy
};
```

3. Add the `toy` entry to `llvm_root_dir/include/llvm/ MC/MCExpr.h`:

```
class MCSymbolRefExpr : public MCExpr {
public:
enum VariantKind {
...
VK_TOY_LO,
VK_TOY_HI,
};
```

4. Add the `toy` entry to `llvm_root_dir/include/llvm/ Support/ELF.h`:

```
enum {
EM_NONE = 0, // No machine
EM_M32 = 1, // AT&T WE 32100
...

...

EM_TOY = 220 // whatever is the next number
};
```

5. Then, add the `toy` entry to `lib/MC/MCExpr.cpp`:

```
StringRef MCSymbolRefExpr::getVariantKindName(VariantKind
Kind) {
switch (Kind) {
...

...

case VK_TOY_LO: return "TOY_LO";
case VK_TOY_HI: return "TOY_HI";
}
...
}
```

6. Next, add the `toy` entry to `lib/Support/Triple.cpp`:

```
const char *Triple::getArchTypeName(ArchType Kind) {
switch (Kind) {
...

...

case toy: return "toy";
}
const char *Triple::getArchTypePrefix(ArchType Kind) {
switch (Kind) {
...

...

case toy: return "toy";
}
}
```

```
Triple::ArchType Triple::getArchTypeForLLVMName(StringRef
Name) {
...
...
.Case("toy", toy)
...
}
static Triple::ArchType parseArch(StringRef ArchName) {
...
...
.Case("toy", Triple::toy)
...
}
static unsigned
getArchPointerBitWidth(llvm::Triple::ArchType Arch) {
...
...
case llvm::Triple::toy:
return 32;
...
...
}
Triple Triple::get32BitArchVariant() const {
...
...
case Triple::toy:
// Already 32-bit.
break;
...
}
Triple Triple::get64BitArchVariant() const {
...
...
case Triple::toy:
T.setArch(UnknownArch);
break;
...
...
}
```

7. Add the toy directory entry to lib/Target/LLVMBuild.txt:

```
[common]
subdirectories = ARM AArch64 CppBackend Hexagon MSP430 ... ...
TOY
```

8. Create a new file called `TOY.h` in the `lib/Target/TOY` folder:

```
#ifndef TARGET_TOY_H
#define TARGET_TOY_H
#include "MCTargetDesc/TOYMCTargetDesc.h"
#include "llvm/Target/TargetMachine.h"
namespace llvm {
class TargetMachine;
class TOYTargetMachine;
FunctionPass *createTOYISelDag(TOYTargetMachine &TM,
                                CodeGenOpt::Level OptLevel);
} // end namespace llvm;
#endif
```

9. Create a new folder called `TargetInfo` in the `lib/Target/TOY` folder. Inside that folder, create a new file called `TOYTargetInfo.cpp`, as follows:

```
#include "TOY.h"
#include "llvm/IR/Module.h"
#include "llvm/Support/TargetRegistry.h"
using namespace llvm;
Target llvm::TheTOYTarget;
extern "C" void LLVMInitializeTOYTargetInfo() {
  RegisterTarget<Triple::toy> X(TheTOYTarget, "toy", "TOY");
}
```

10. In the same folder, create the `CMakeLists.txt` file:

```
add_llvm_library(LLVMTOYInfo TOYTargetInfo.cpp)
```

11. Create an `LLVMBuild.txt` file:

```
[component_0]
type = Library
name = TOYInfo
parent = TOY
required_libraries = Support
add_to_library_groups = TOY
```

12. In the `lib/Target/TOY` folder, create a file called `TOYTargetMachine.cpp`:

```
#include "TOYTargetMachine.h"
#include "TOY.h"
#include "TOYFrameLowering.h"
#include "TOYInstrInfo.h"
#include "TOYISelLowering.h "
#include "TOYSelectionDAGInfo.h"
#include "llvm/CodeGen/Passes.h"
#include "llvm/IR/Module.h"
```

```
#include "llvm/PassManager.h"
#include "llvm/Support/TargetRegistry.h"
using namespace llvm;

TOYTargetMachine::TOYTargetMachine(const Target &T, StringRef TT,
StringRef CPU, StringRef FS, const
TargetOptions &Options, Reloc::Model RM,
CodeModel::Model CM, CodeGenOpt::Level OL)
    : LLVMTargetMachine(T, TT, CPU, FS, Options, RM, CM, OL),
      Subtarget(TT, CPU, FS, *this) {
  initAsmInfo();
}

namespace {
class TOYPassConfig : public TargetPassConfig {
public:
  TOYPassConfig(TOYTargetMachine *TM, PassManagerBase &PM)
      : TargetPassConfig(TM, PM) {}
  TOYTargetMachine &getTOYTargetMachine() const {
    return getTM<TOYTargetMachine>();
  }
  virtual bool addPreISel();
  virtual bool addInstSelector();
  virtual bool addPreEmitPass();
};
} // namespace

TargetPassConfig *TOYTargetMachine::createPassConfig
(PassManagerBase &PM) {
  return new TOYPassConfig(this, PM);
}

bool TOYPassConfig::addPreISel() { return false; }

bool TOYPassConfig::addInstSelector() {
  addPass(createTOYISelDag(getTOYTargetMachine(),
getOptLevel()));
  return false;
}

bool TOYPassConfig::addPreEmitPass() { return false; }

// Force static initialization.
extern "C" void LLVMInitializeTOYTarget() {
```

```
    RegisterTargetMachine<TOYTargetMachine> X(TheTOYTarget);
}
void TOYTargetMachine::addAnalysisPasses(PassManagerBase &PM) {}
```

13. Create a new folder called `MCTargetDesc` and a new file called
    `TOYMCTargetDesc.h`:

```
#ifndef TOYMCTARGETDESC_H
#define TOYMCTARGETDESC_H
#include "llvm/Support/DataTypes.h"
namespace llvm {
class Target;
class MCInstrInfo;
class MCRegisterInfo;
class MCSubtargetInfo;
class MCContext;
class MCCodeEmitter;
class MCAsmInfo;
class MCCodeGenInfo;
class MCInstPrinter;
class MCObjectWriter;
class MCAsmBackend;
class StringRef;
class raw_ostream;
extern Target TheTOYTarget;

MCCodeEmitter *createTOYMCCodeEmitter(const MCInstrInfo &MCII,
const MCRegisterInfo &MRI, const MCSubtargetInfo &STI, MCContext
&Ctx);

MCAsmBackend *createTOYAsmBackend(const Target &T, const
MCRegisterInfo &MRI, StringRef TT, StringRef CPU);

MCObjectWriter *createTOYELFObjectWriter(raw_ostream &OS, uint8_t
OSABI);
} // End llvm namespace
#define GET_REGINFO_ENUM
#include "TOYGenRegisterInfo.inc"
#define GET_INSTRINFO_ENUM
#include "TOYGenInstrInfo.inc"
#define GET_SUBTARGETINFO_ENUM
#include "TOYGenSubtargetInfo.inc"
#endif
```

14. Create one more file, called `TOYMCTargetDesc.cpp`, in the same folder:

```cpp
#include "TOYMCTargetDesc.h"
#include "InstPrinter/TOYInstPrinter.h"
#include "TOYMCAsmInfo.h"
#include "llvm/MC/MCCodeGenInfo.h"
#include "llvm/MC/MCInstrInfo.h"
#include "llvm/MC/MCRegisterInfo.h"
#include "llvm/MC/MCSubtargetInfo.h"
#include "llvm/MC/MCStreamer.h"
#include "llvm/Support/ErrorHandling.h"
#include "llvm/Support/FormattedStream.h"
#include "llvm/Support/TargetRegistry.h"
#define GET_INSTRINFO_MC_DESC
#include "TOYGenInstrInfo.inc"
#define GET_SUBTARGETINFO_MC_DESC
#include "TOYGenSubtargetInfo.inc"
#define GET_REGINFO_MC_DESC
#include "TOYGenRegisterInfo.inc"
using namespace llvm;

static MCInstrInfo *createTOYMCInstrInfo() {
  MCInstrInfo *X = new MCInstrInfo();
  InitTOYMCInstrInfo(X);
  return X;
}

static MCRegisterInfo *createTOYMCRegisterInfo(StringRef TT) {
  MCRegisterInfo *X = new MCRegisterInfo();
  InitTOYMCRegisterInfo(X, TOY::LR);
  return X;
}

static MCSubtargetInfo *createTOYMCSubtargetInfo(StringRef TT,
StringRef CPU, StringRef FS) {
  MCSubtargetInfo *X = new MCSubtargetInfo();
  InitTOYMCSubtargetInfo(X, TT, CPU, FS);
  return X;
}

static MCAsmInfo *createTOYMCAsmInfo(const MCRegisterInfo &MRI,
StringRef TT) {
  MCAsmInfo *MAI = new TOYMCAsmInfo(TT);
  return MAI;
}
```

```
static MCCodeGenInfo *createTOYMCCodeGenInfo(StringRef TT,
Reloc::Model RM, CodeModel::Model CM, CodeGenOpt::Level OL)
  {
  MCCodeGenInfo *X = new MCCodeGenInfo();
  if (RM == Reloc::Default) {
    RM = Reloc::Static;
  }
  if (CM == CodeModel::Default) {
    CM = CodeModel::Small;
  }
  if (CM != CodeModel::Small && CM != CodeModel::Large) {
    report_fatal_error("Target only supports CodeModel Small or
Large");
  }
  X->InitMCCodeGenInfo(RM, CM, OL);
  return X;
}


static MCInstPrinter *
createTOYMCInstPrinter(const Target &T, unsigned SyntaxVariant,
                       const MCAsmInfo &MAI, const MCInstrInfo &
MII, const MCRegisterInfo &MRI, const MCSubtargetInfo &STI) {
  return new TOYInstPrinter(MAI, MII, MRI);
}


static MCStreamer *
createMCAsmStreamer(MCContext &Ctx, formatted_raw_ostream &OS,
                    bool isVerboseAsm, bool useDwarfDirectory,
                    MCInstPrinter *InstPrint, MCCodeEmitter *CE,
                    MCAsmBackend *TAB, bool ShowInst) {
  return createAsmStreamer(Ctx, OS, isVerboseAsm, useD -
  warfDirectory, InstPrint, CE, TAB, ShowInst);
}


static MCStreamer *createMCStreamer(const Target &T, StringRef TT,
MCContext &Ctx, MCAsmBackend &MAB, raw_ostream &OS,
MCCodeEmitter *Emitter, const MCSubtargetInfo &STI,
bool RelaxAll, bool NoExecStack) {
  return createELFStreamer(Ctx, MAB, OS, Emitter, false,
NoExecStack);
}


// Force static initialization.
extern "C" void LLVMInitializeTOYTargetMC() {
  // Register the MC asm info.
```

```
   RegisterMCAsmInfoFn X(TheTOYTarget, createTOYMCAsmInfo);
   // Register the MC codegen info.
   TargetRegistry::RegisterMCCodeGenInfo(TheTOYTarget,
createTOYMCCodeGenInfo);
   // Register the MC instruction info.
   TargetRegistry::RegisterMCInstrInfo(TheTOYTarget,
createTOYMCInstrInfo);
   // Register the MC register info.
   TargetRegistry::RegisterMCRegInfo(TheTOYTarget,
createTOYMCRegisterInfo);
   // Register the MC subtarget info.
   TargetRegistry::RegisterMCSubtargetInfo(TheTOYTarget,
                                           createTOYMCSub
targetInfo);
   // Register the MCInstPrinter
   TargetRegistry::RegisterMCInstPrinter(TheTOYTarget,
createTOYMCInstPrinter);
   // Register the ASM Backend.
   TargetRegistry::RegisterMCAsmBackend(TheTOYTarget,
createTOYAsmBackend);
   // Register the assembly streamer.
   TargetRegistry::RegisterAsmStreamer(TheTOYTarget,
createMCAsmStreamer);
   // Register the object streamer.
   TargetRegistry::RegisterMCObjectStreamer(TheTOYTarget,
createMCStreamer);
   // Register the MCCodeEmitter
   TargetRegistry::RegisterMCCodeEmitter(TheTOYTarget,
createTOYMCCodeEmitter);
   }
```

15. In the same folder, create an `LLVMBuild.txt` file:

```
[component_0]
type = Library
name = TOYDesc
parent = TOY
required_libraries = MC Support TOYAsmPrinter TOYInfo
add_to_library_groups = TOY
```

16. Create a CMakeLists.txt file:

```
add_llvm_library(LLVMTOYDesc
TOYMCTargetDesc.cpp)
```

Build the enitre LLVM project, as follows:

```
$ cmake llvm_src_dir -DCMAKE_BUILD_TYPE=Release -
DLLVM_TARGETS_TO_BUILD="TOY"
$ make


Here, we have specified that we are building the LLVM compiler for
the toy target. After the build completes, check whether the TOY
target appears with the llc command:
$ llc -version
...

...

Registered Targets :
toy - TOY
```

The following IR, when given to the llc tool, will generate an assembly as shown:

```
target datalayout = "e-m:e-p:32:32-i1:8:32-i8:8:32- i16:16:32-i64:32-
f64:32-a:0:32-n32"
target triple = "toy"
define i32 @foo(i32 %a, i32 %b){
  %c = add nsw i32 %a, %b
  ret i32 %c
}


$ llc foo.ll

.text
.file "foo.ll"
.globl foo
.type foo,@function
foo: # @foo
# BB#0: # %entry
add r0, r0, r1
b lr
.Ltmp0:
.size foo, .Ltmp0-foo
```

To see the details of how to register a target with llc, you can visit http://llvm. org/docs/WritingAnLLVMBackend.html#target-registration and http:// jonathan2251.github.io/lbd/llvmstructure.html#target-registration by Chen Chung-Shu and Anoushe Jamshidi.

Summary

In this chapter, we had a brief discussion about how a target architecture machine can be represented in LLVM. We saw the ease of using tablegen in organizing data such as register sets, instruction sets, calling conventions, and so on, for a given target. The llvm-tablegen then converts these target descriptor .td fies into enums, which can be used in program logic such as frame lowering, instruction selection, instruction printing, and so on. More detailed and complex architectures like ARM and X86 can give insight on a detailed description of the target.

In the first chapter, we tried a basic exercise to get hands-on with various tools provided by the LLVM infrastructure. In the subsequent chapters, that is, *Chapter 2, Building LLVM IR*, and *Chapter 3, Advanced LLVM IR*, we used APIs provided by LLVM to emit IRs. Readers can use those APIs in their frontend to convert their language to LLVM IR. In *Chapter 5, Advanced IR Block Transformations*, we got used to Pass Pipeline for IR optimization and went through some examples. In *Chapter 6, IR to Selection DAG Phase*, readers got familiar with the conversion of IR to selection DAG, which is a step towards emitting machine code. In this final chapter, we saw how to represent sample architecture with tablegen and use it for emitting code.

After reading this book, we hope that readers become familiar with LLVM infrastructure and are ready to dive deeply into LLVM and create compilers on their own for their custom architecture or a custom language. Happy Compiling!

Index

memory access operations 37, 38
memory location
  writing into 43-45
methods, for filling information
  AnalysisUsage::addPreserved<>
      method 62
  AnalysisUsage::addRequired<> method 62
  AnalysisUsage:addRequiredTransitive<>
      method 62
methods, for instruction simplification
  SimplifyAddInst 64
  SimplifyAndInst 64
  SimplifyBinOp 63
  SimplifySubInst 64
methods, for simplification of
    instcombine module
  SimplifyAssociativeOrCommutative 66
  tryFactorization 66
modular design 2, 3
module
  function, emitting in 13, 14
ModulePass subclass 56

N

natural loops 72

O

opt
  about 9
  command line arguments 9
Optimizer 2

P

Pass class
  about 56-61
  virtual methods 57
passes
  reference link 54
Pass info
  using, in own Pass 61, 62
Pass Manager class
  about 56-61
  flags 61

PBQP Register Allocator 113
PHI instruction 25

R

register allocated local variables 5
register allocation 112
register allocation, for mapping virtual
    registers to physical registers
  Direct Mapping 112
  Indirect Mapping 112
register allocation techniques, LLVM
  Basic Register Allocator 113
  Fast Register Allocator 113
  Greedy Register Allocator 113
  PBQP Register Allocator 113
registers
  defining 118, 119
registers set
  defining 118, 119
return statement
  emitting 18, 19

S

sample backend
  about 118
  calling convention, defining 119, 120
  registers, defining 118, 119
  registers sets, defining 118, 119
scalar
  extracting, from vector 48-50
  inserting, into vector 45-48
scalar evolution 75-77
Scalar Evolution Optimization 69
selectionDAG
  about 117
  IR, converting to 98-101
  legalizing 102, 103
  optimizing 103-106
simple arithmetic statement
  emitting, in basic block 22-24
single instruction multiple data (SIMD) 45
SLP Vectorization 80
spilling 112

stack allocated local variables 5
static single assignment (SSA) 5
Superword-Level Parallelism (SLP) 79

T

tablegen tool
  about 3, 118
  reference link 118
TargetTransformInfo (TTI) 87

V

vector
  scalar, extracting from 48-50
  scalar, inserting into 45-48
vectorization 79-89
virtual methods, Pass class
  doFinalization 57
  doInitialization 57
  runOn{Passtype} 57

Thank you for buying
LLVM Essentials

About Packt Publishing

Packt, pronounced 'packed', published its first book, *Mastering phpMyAdmin for Effective MySQL Management*, in April 2004, and subsequently continued to specialize in publishing highly focused books on specific technologies and solutions.

Our books and publications share the experiences of your fellow IT professionals in adapting and customizing today's systems, applications, and frameworks. Our solution-based books give you the knowledge and power to customize the software and technologies you're using to get the job done. Packt books are more specific and less general than the IT books you have seen in the past. Our unique business model allows us to bring you more focused information, giving you more of what you need to know, and less of what you don't.

Packt is a modern yet unique publishing company that focuses on producing quality, cutting-edge books for communities of developers, administrators, and newbies alike. For more information, please visit our website at www.packtpub.com.

About Packt Open Source

In 2010, Packt launched two new brands, Packt Open Source and Packt Enterprise, in order to continue its focus on specialization. This book is part of the Packt Open Source brand, home to books published on software built around open source licenses, and offering information to anybody from advanced developers to budding web designers. The Open Source brand also runs Packt's Open Source Royalty Scheme, by which Packt gives a royalty to each open source project about whose software a book is sold.

Writing for Packt

We welcome all inquiries from people who are interested in authoring. Book proposals should be sent to author@packtpub.com. If your book idea is still at an early stage and you would like to discuss it first before writing a formal book proposal, then please contact us; one of our commissioning editors will get in touch with you.

We're not just looking for published authors; if you have strong technical skills but no writing experience, our experienced editors can help you develop a writing career, or simply get some additional reward for your expertise.

Getting Started with LLVM Core Libraries

Get to grips with LLVM essentials and use the core libraries to build advanced tools

Bruno Cardoso Lopes Rafael Auler PACKT open source ✤

Getting Started with LLVM Core Libraries

ISBN: 978-1-78216-692-4   Paperback: 314 pages

Get to grips with LLVM essentials and use the core libraries to build advanced tools

1. Learn how to configure, build, and use LLVM and Clang based tools.

2. Explore the depths of the LLVM front-end, IR, code generator, and libraries, and learn how a modern compiler is implemented in a practical way.

3. Customize your project to benefit from Just in Time compilation (JIT), static analysis and source-to-source transformations.

Quick answers to common problems

LLVM Cookbook

Over 80 engaging recipes that will help you build a compiler frontend, optimizer, and code generator using LLVM

Mayur Pandey Suyog Sarda [ ] open source

LLVM Cookbook

ISBN: 978-1-78528-598-1   Paperback: 296 pages

Over 80 engaging recipes that will help you build a compiler frontend, optimizer, and code generator using LLVM

1. Write a frontend for any language to generate LLVM IR.

2. Create optimization passes to optimize the IR code using LLVM Pass Infrastructure and Pass Manager.

3. Design and implement structures for highly-optimized compilers using LLVM, through detailed step-by-step recipes.

Please check **www.PacktPub.com** for information on our titles

Game Development with SlimDX

ISBN: 978-1-78216-738-9   Paperback: 150 pages

A fast-paced and practical guide on game development using SlimDX

1. Harness the power of DirectInput and XInput to detect and respond to user input from keyboard, mouse, and joysticks/gamepads while adding the allimportant interactivity to your games.

2. Make the most of Direct2D, DirectSound, XAudio2, and Direct3D to make your game worlds come to life on the screen.

3. A practical guide packed with example code and quick instructions on game development with SlimDX.

LÖVE for Lua Game Programming

ISBN: 978-1-78216-160-8   Paperback: 106 pages

Master the Lua programming language and build exciting strategy-based games in 2D using the LÖVE framework

1. Discover the LÖVE framework and build games easily and efficiently.

2. Learn how to utilize the LÖVE framework's tools to create a 2D game world.

3. A step-by-step approach to learning game development.

Please check **www.PacktPub.com** for information on our titles

CPSIA information can be obtained at www.ICGtesting.com
Printed in the USA
LVOW09s2326211215

467401LV00010B/436/P